Where Eagles Rest

Hyrum W. Smith

Covenant
Communications, Inc.

First Printing, 1982
Printed in the United States of America
Second Printing, 1990
Covenant Communications, Inc.
Library of Congress Catalog Card number 89-082278
ISBN 1-55503-217-6

CONTENTS

PREFACE

My reasons for writing this book started with my own keen interests. I remember as a boy taking one chore at a time and coming up with faster and better ways of doing it without lessening the quality of the work. When I was on my mission, I had to learn what it takes to be a successful missionary. Shortly after my mission I was drafted into the army. One of my lasting impressions of the military was the simple, yet thorough, nature of its basic training program. The whole purpose was to teach a soldier to survive under tremendous stress.

Later, as a mission president, I had the opportunity to reflect in depth, particularly as I witnessed the struggles of some six hundred missionaries, on the urgency of basic training for spiritual survival. The result of those reflections is *Where Eagles Rest*. Within each of the chapters, I expand upon a principle I consider to be a key to individual survival which was also exemplified in the life of the Savior.

I consider positive change essential to personal growth, and growth becomes more effective as we discover who we are. I have suggested two perspectives from which to view oneself: eternal and historical. Paying attention to the cues we receive from our eternal heritage assists us in our own self-discovery.

However, being aware of true principles is only a small part of winning the battle for our eternal birthright. Unwavering obedience to true principles will ultimately determine our celestial opportunities.

The Lord has given us what I call his laundry lists

to help us keep our own linen clean. Positive changes will occur only when we set goals and personally commit to their accomplishment through specific plans of action.

If we listen and pay careful attention during basic training experiences, we can make it when the real tests come. I believe *Where Eagles Rest* comes close to a "how-to-do-it" basic training manual. It does not have all the answers. I am solely responsible for the interpretations of doctrine and history.

May the Lord bless you, not only to become further aware of the basic training necessary for your survival, but that you will be willing to internalize and implement the principles which will bring you eternal happiness.

Hyrum W. Smith

WHERE EAGLES REST

Climbing higher, reaching upward,
Ever soaring on.
Mighty eagle—stretching out your wings to fly
For the sky.
Dare to be an eagle free.
Dare to fly an eagle high.
Dare yourself, oh dare yourself to see,
Dare to be.
Through the blue sky heading for the sun,
See the light ahead.
With desire you can make that wish come true—
It's up to you.

Dare to dream an eagle's dream.
Dare to fly on your own wings.
Dare yourself, oh dare yourself to be,
Dare to reach.
See the vision of what you can be—
You're a child of God.
Choicest spirit—everlasting destiny
Waits for thee.

Dare to rest where eagles rest.
Know you've done your very best.
With your Father you'll eternally be.
Dare to see.

Dare to rest where eagles rest.
Know you've done your very best.
With our Father we'll eternally be,
Dare to see
Where eagles rest.

Karen Worthington

EYE OF FAITH

**Seeing ourselves as we want to be is a key
to personal growth**

I have been very concerned with the issue of
change in our lives, why we need change, and how
change is wrought in our lives, particularly when we
want to change ourselves.

The Mission of Alma to the People of Zarahemla

In the fifth chapter of Alma in the *Book of Mormon*,
Alma goes to the city of Zarahemla and begins to
preach. He has given up his judgeship and he goes
there because the people have become corrupt.

Alma begins to chew the people out. This is one
of the greatest chapters of "chewing outs" I have ever
read. It's a great conference talk. If you feel you need
a good chewing out, read the fifth chapter of Alma.

In verse fourteen Alma starts to get warmed up.
He asks the people three powerful questions: (1) "Now,
behold, I ask you, my brethren of the church, have ye
been spiritually born of God? (2) Have ye received his
image in your countenances? (3) Have ye experienced
this mighty change in your hearts?"

I found those very interesting questions. Let's suppose I'm Alma just railing at you. How would you respond to those three questions: Have you spiritually
been born of God? Have you received His image in your

countenance? (—which means, are you becoming like Him, are you beginning to look like Him?) And, have you experienced this mighty change in your heart?

It's that change that I would like to discuss. Whatever we are doing now, whatever our progress or track record has been up till now, if we want that to change, *we've got to change.* For example, if you are a B student and that's been your average, if you don't want to graduate as a B student, something has to change. If you continue to do pretty much what you have been doing in the past, you'll be a B student forever.

Identifying the change and then making something happen are very difficult things. I would like to share with you a system for creating change in your life. Across the page in chapter five, Alma asks another question. You should understand that the people of Zarahemla are members of the church who have gotten off the track.

"Now behold, I say unto you, my brethren, if ye have experienced a change of heart, and if ye have felt to sing the song of redeeming love"—in other words, if you have gone through some of these changes—*"can ye feel so now?"* Can you still feel the change? Alma really lowered his artillery with that one.

He knew the response to the question would be negative because they had gotten off the track. Well, we have to ask ourselves, "Can we still feel it now?" If at one time we felt an experience with the Holy Ghost, are we still experiencing those feelings? And if not, why not?

Missions Change People

Sometimes we'll hear a returned missionary talk about the awful transition he went through when he came home from his mission.

We know that transitions are not necessary for missionaries when they come home. Missionaries change in the mission field. Why? Because they recognize they can't do it by themselves and they get help from their Father in Heaven. They pray a lot. They study the scriptures a lot. And this causes change. They come home; they're different.

But many of them, when they get home, stop praying often every day, stop studying the scriptures every day, and then wonder why they go through a spiritual let-down when they get home from their missions.

We will hear many of them say, "Boy, I really miss the missionary spirit." Well, they don't ever have to miss the missionary spirit if they continue to do at home what they did in the mission field.

The Story of the Brother of Jared

Do you remember the experience that the brother of Jared had with the rocks in the second and third chapters of Ether? That is a great, powerful story, and it illustrates the principle that I'm going to teach.

The brother of Jared came to the seashore, as you recall, and wanted to know why he was there. He said, "Lord, here we are at the coast, why are we here?"

The Lord said, "You're going to build some boats and take your people across the ocean to the Promised Land."

"But Lord, I don't know how to build boats."

"I know that. I'm going to teach you how."

"Fine."

So the Lord instructed the brother of Jared.

He built eight boats. After he built the boats, he stepped back, looked at them, and said, "You know, Lord, those are the strangest looking boats I've ever

seen. There is no way for air to get into these boats."
(Remember they were built like a dish.) "Not only that,
there is no light in the boats. We'll perish going across
the ocean."

Now the Lord was very patient with the brother
of Jared. He said, "Well, if you want air, cut a hole in
the bottom and cut a hole in the top, and then put a
plug in each hole, and when you're out on the ocean,
unplug one of the corks. If water rushes in, that's the
wrong hole."

I'm paraphrasing, but the basic story is correct. The
brother of Jared then said, "How are we going to get
light?"

Then the Lord said an interesting thing. "What
would you have me do about it?" He didn't come
sliding down a sunbeam, like the cosmic slave some
think he is, and say, "Poof, here's your light." What he
did say was this, "What would you have me do about
it?"

The brother of Jared answered, "Give me a little
time and I'll be back."

So he went out; and with his eye of faith, he decided that, if he would create sixteen rocks and if the Lord
would touch those rocks, he'd have light. He saw those
rocks all lit up with his eye of faith.

With the eye of faith, he went out and "molten"
the rocks, brought them back, and laid them upon the
ground. "Lord, you wanted to know what I wanted you
to do. Touch my rocks and we will have light."

The Savior stretched forth his finger and touched
each of the rocks. And while he was doing that, the
brother of Jared saw the finger of the Lord, and it scared
him. He fell to the ground, all bunched up; and while
the Lord was touching the rocks, he looked over and
saw the brother of Jared all curled up and said, "What
is the matter?"

And the brother of Jared said, "I saw your finger and I was afraid that you would smite me."

Then the Savior said a fascinating thing. "What else did you see?"

"That's all; just a finger."

And then the Lord said, "Brother of Jared, no one has had more faith than you have and because of your faith, I have to show you the rest of me." The Savior didn't say, "I would like to show you the rest," nor "it would be neat for you to see the rest." He said, "I have to show you the rest." And then he displayed himself in his majesty to the brother of Jared.

There are two powerful lessons we learn from that experience. One, *we have to do something first;* we have to exercise our faith. Exercising faith is mental and physical exertion. We've got to do something. Two, *there is a level of faith,* a plateau of faith, at which the Lord cannot withhold himself from our view. There is natural law in play that says, "If you have faith like the brother of Jared, the Savior has to appear to you." He has to; the *Doctrine and Covenants* teaches that. The 107th section, verses eighteen and nineteen, tells us about the Melchizedek Priesthood and the blessings which are available as a result of that priesthood.

Because the brother of Jared had the ability to see with his eye of faith, those rocks lit up; a miracle occurred.

A System of Change

To successfully bring about change in our lives, we need to implement a system of change that is built upon three assumptions, and then identify how we can become more like the Savior. If you will apply this system, I promise you that you can become the kind of person you want to become.

First assumption: We change our lives by changing the attitudes of our minds.

Second assumption: We become what we think
about all day long.

Third assumption: Our mind is naturally goal
seeking.

Please remember these assumptions. Our mind is always trying to accomplish something. We have a powerful machine wanting to achieve goals. It will set the goals that we allow it to.

Based upon these three assumptions, we *will* build a model for change. Imagine a blank sheet of paper with a circle in the center. Draw through the circle several spokes, say twenty spokes. The center of that circle represents you and me, and the lines (spokes) through that circle represent the roles that we play each day in our lives. What are some of the different roles we play? *Student* is a role. What is another? *Mother, father.* What are other roles we play? *Teacher, friend, sibling, husband, cook, driver.* There are many different roles that we play each day. We could list hundreds of them.

For the sake of this experience, isolate the role of *missionary.* Are we not all expected to be missionaries? We are! Let us isolate that role and see how we are doing in that particular area.

Imagine a line from top to bottom on another piece of paper. The top of that line represents the ultimate missionary; that's Ammon. Remember Ammon? He was great. He baptized thousands. A successful fourteen-year mission. Phenomenal!

At the bottom of the line, performance as a missionary is not so hot. Somewhere between the bottom and the top is our performance as a missionary. Let's say our actual performance is just above the center. Our self-image as a missionary will always be on the upper edge of actual performance. In other words, we perform at a point several spaces below the point we think we are performing.

For example, at least once a week, we walk across the street, tell our neighbor we love him, and invite him for a family home evening. We do that every week, never miss. That means our performance level is at the point just above center. Sometimes our visit is every two weeks. Our performance point is now lower. When we visit every three weeks our performance level has dropped below the center point. If we want to change our performance in this particular role for the better, we have to move our self-image of that performance up the line. You can apply this system of change for any role you play, and there are lots of them.

We have to see ourselves performing at the higher level to improve our actual performance. If we can do that, the performance *will* follow. Now the question is if we want to do that, how do we do it? There are two ways. We have to attack our *self-talking* and our *self-thinking*.

What are we doing? We are trying to move our self-image in that role up the spectrum of performance. We have to attack what we *think* about ourselves and what we *say* about ourselves. How do we do that? How do we specifically attack our self-talking and our self-thinking? The answer is we use *constructive imagination*. Do you know what constructive imagination is? It is the eye of faith. It is having an eye single to the glory of God. With an eye of faith like the brother of Jared, it is seeing ourselves doing what Ammon did. What did Ammon do? He didn't mess around with the villagers; he went and converted the king. A great way to baptize.

It can happen today. I had a Samoan friend, Al Harrington, whom I grew up with in Hawaii. He is a magnificent human being. He went to Samoa on his mission. They are still under the Matain system which means they still have the king and queen form of government. He'd baptize the king, and the king would bring his whole village with him into the church. The mission got my friend a bus because he was baptizing hundreds of people. Great program!

He had to see himself laboring there first. Constructive imagination is that eye of faith. We want to be a pianist; we have to see ourselves with the eye of faith playing the piano. It consists of three parts.

Constructive Imagination

Verbal: *The words we say to ourselves and about ourselves.*

Visual: *What we see ourselves doing.*

Emotional: *What we feel about ourselves.*

Now, what are we doing to initiate change? We are attacking our *self-talking* and *self-thinking*. How? With constructive imagination. What is constructive imagination? It is what we say *to* and *about* ourselves. It is what *we* see ourselves doing. It is what we *feel* about ourselves.

If we can somehow change so that we are improving what we see, feel, and say about ourselves, then something is going to change. Something different is going to happen.

There are three things which I am going to ask you to do which are necessary in implementing construction imagination.

| *First:* | *Choose the characteristic or skills you want to change.* |

We have already identified missionary work. You may be a student. You may be a father or a mother. Choose the skill or activity you want to change or to improve. We are not going to go into all the things in missionary work we could change, let's just leave it at missionary work.

| *Second:* | *Define exactly what kind of image we want (the depth of change).* |

After we select the role in which we want to improve and have specifically identified those areas of improvement, we define the depth of the improvement; we say what kind of missionary do we want to see ourselves being? Do we want to be like a LeGrand Richards? He is just great. He has always been a missionary. Can we see ourselves doing what LeGrand Richards has done?

The second part of the specifics of constructive imagination, once we've identified the role, is to define the depth of the imagined change which we want to portray.

| *Third:* | *Write the affirmation.* |

We have identified the role and defined the depth of change, now we have to write an affirmation which describes our fulfilling the role. What is an affirmation?

| *An affirmation:* | *is a positive, constructive statement describing us as if the change has already taken place.* |

We are going to write it as if we are that way now. Let me give you the rules for writing affirmations, then give you some examples of affirmation, and finally discuss how we use them.

Writing Affirmations

First rule:	*They must be positive.*
Second rule:	*They must be personal. Use I or we.*
Third rule:	*Use the present tense. Assume the change has already taken place.*
Fourth rule:	*Don't compare yourself with others.*
Fifth rule:	*Describe an activity rather than an ability.*
Sixth rule:	*They must be realistic.*

The summary of these six rules is this: Imagine that we have already made the change that we want to make.

As I give you some examples of affirmations, this concept will make more sense. Let's say, as full-time missionaries, we want to improve our ability to tract. Here is the affirmation: "I tract very effectively, knowing that I have a great message, and thrill when I follow in the footsteps of Christ." That is an affirmation.

I may not be anywhere near that level of performance yet. I may be absolutely scared to death. Have you ever gone tracting? Tracting is a scary experience. We have to knock on somebody's door and try and talk them into listening to us. We have to try and convince them, because they don't want to listen to us automatically. It's an experience in rejection. Have you ever had an experience with rejection? There are all kinds. What happens when we have a bitter experience with somebody? Somebody casts us out. What is the natural human response? We run home, leap into bed, assume the fetal position, and turn the electric blanket up to nine.

If we had a bad experience, we don't want to repeat it. What do we really need to do? We need to leap to the next door, don't we? And get thrown out again.

To improve in this area we need to write an affirmation that describes us already there. Here is another example: "I teach with power and authority because I am well prepared through regular study of the scriptures, fervent prayer, and constant review of the gospel." We don't write, "I'm going to be teaching *later on* with power and authority," but, "I teach with power and authority *now!*" Do you begin to see what I am getting at?

Why are we *writing affirmations*? Because we want to attack our self-thinking and our self-talking. Why? Because we need to improve our self-image. If we never change our self-image, we do not change the performance. It will not change. So we are going to attack that. So, how? We are going to use constructive imagination.

Remember, constructive imagination has three parts: verbal, visual, and emotional. Specifically, what do we do? We define the role we want to change, exactly how we want to change, and then we have an affirmation describing the change.

Let's say we have taken the time to write eight or ten affirmations for the role we are going to change in our lives.

What do we do with the affirmations now that we have written them? We are going to do three things.

Do you notice how we deal in threes? I am going to ask you to do three things with these affirmations.

Putting Affirmations into Practice

Number One: *Read them every night for six months.*

After we have written them on three-by-five cards or in our little black book, we read them every night for six months. Do you know how long six months is? For a missionary, it's forever. Six months is a long time. Read those affirmations every night for six months.

Do you remember those three basic assumptions that we started with? We become what we think about all day long. Read the affirmations every night for six months.

Number Two: *See yourself experiencing the activity from the inside, not as a spectator.*

With the eye of faith, see yourself experiencing the activity from inside, not as a spectator. Now, that is important. If we want to see ourselves as a powerful teacher, we have to see ourselves actually teaching with power and authority. It is not like we watch television, "Look at me teach, aren't I great?" Not that. We must see ourselves and the situation through our own eyes actually teaching with power and authority. We have to see ourselves in that manner to achieve the desired results. That is the second thing we do with our affirmation.

Number Three: *Feel the positive emotion and pleasure which come from the activity.*

If we will do those three things every night with whatever we want to change in our life, the change will occur.

Do we want to be a successful business person? Do we want to be a great doctor, or dentist, or whatever? We have to see ourselves there—not in a general way, but in a very specific way. We have to change how we feel about ourselves inside. There is an interesting exercise that will get you started.

The Number Ten Exercise

In the center of a clean sheet of paper draw a circle the size of a fifty-cent piece. Now write the word *you* in that circle. This represents you, the human being. From this center circle draw ten to twelve spokes about two inches long. At the end of each spoke draw another circle about the size of a quarter. In each of these outer circles, identify one of the roles you play each day. For example: father, mother, friend, brother, sister, teacher, employee, student, missionary, cook, and so forth. There are literally hundreds of different roles you play. The ten or twelve spokes you have identified will do for this exercise.

Next, review each of the roles you have identified. Measure your performance in that role on a scale from one to ten—one being very poor, ten being the best, celestial, on the edge of being translated. Put that number in each of the outer circles.

Think to yourself, "What kind of friend am I on a scale from one to ten?" Then write that number in the outer circle which you have labeled "friend." This, by the way, is a marvelous family home evening activity.

Repeat this for each of the roles you have selected. Now that you have all the outer circles thus numbered, there is one more assignment. Do the same thing in the center circle marked *you*. On a scale from one to ten, indicate what kind of a human being you are. Put that number in the center circle. This how you rate yourself as a human being.

Let me now make what I call an impact statement. *If you did not put a ten in the center circle, you do not have the capacity to be a ten in any of the outer circles.* What point am I making? The Lord did not make a seven or eight or even a nine person. *All He made were tens!* This is not an arrogant, conceited, offensive thing to say. It is a quiet, powerful assurance of knowing who you are! You are a son or daughter of God! We are not tens in our roles as yet. That is why we have the mortal experience—the growing to perfection in our roles. As people we are tens.

If you did not place a ten in the center circle, you have until the end of this chapter to get it there! Do you understand? I'm very serious about this. All the affirmations in the world will not work unless you have really, emotionally, spiritually, and mentally placed a ten on the *you* circle.

At the beginning of this chapter, I expressed my concern with change. We have discussed a system of change that works. In the following chapters are basic principles which the Savior exemplified in His life and ministry. I share these principles with you, hoping that you may incorporate them into your daily living, thereby becoming more Christ-like and experiencing more happiness.

You will find at the end of each chapter, beginning with this one, an affirmation dealing with the basic principle discussed in that chapter. I hope they may be a starting point for you as you implement change in your life.

> *I am a ten human being. I came to this earth with the power to become a God and accomplish anything I choose to do.*

EAGLES

Self-discovery is the key to positive change in our self-image.

Discovering who we are and who we can become is an inner desire of us all. We learn something about ourselves from an event in the life of Moses.

Moses Talks with the Lord.

In the first chapter of Moses is recorded a conversation between the Lord and Moses. The Lord had Moses taken to a high mountain and appeared unto him. He had three magnificent things to say to Moses. He began by introducing himself by saying, "I am God." Then he revealed the relationship between himself and Moses by saying, "Thou [Moses] art my son." And He then gave Moses a charge, "I have a work for thee [to do]."

Is there anything Moses couldn't do, knowing that? We would be given the same answer. The Lord is God. We are his sons and daughters, and He has a work for us to do. Is there anything we can't do, knowing that? Why do we limit ourselves? If we're going to act as a son or daughter of God, we have to learn how. These two stories about the eagle tell about who we are, who we can become, and why we are here now. The first is a true story.

The Eagle's Nest

Eagles are fascinating birds to me. Some of them have wing spans of six feet. They are big, magnificent birds.

When they build their nests, they fly to very high places, the tallest trees, or on a high mountain or cliff. The eagle builds a wide nest, and these nests are sometimes four to five feet across. The materials are somewhat different from those used by most birds. They take long, sharp sticks and weave these sticks together so they all poke straight up through the nest. If we were to look at the foundation of it, it would appear to be a very uncomfortable place to live.

After the base is built, the mother eagle flies out and gets leaves, feathers, and grass, and brings them back to weave into these sticks. The feathers and down and other materials come up above the sticks.

Then the eagle lays the eggs. Only one or two eaglets will survive. These two eaglets break out of the egg and they find themselves in this soft, magnificent place. Mom goes out every day and brings back food. They don't have to worry about anything except food and if Mom has come back.

The eaglets grow and soon Mom knows it is time for the eagles to get out of the nest. The mother eagle now does a very interesting thing. Each day she starts to pull the grass from the nest with the feathers and leaves. After a few days, home is quite uncomfortable for the baby eaglets. They find themselves on these sharp sticks, and it is very annoying.

They say, "Gee, Mom, this isn't like it used to be. What a bummer home is. You mean we have to clean our room and do all that other stuff?"

When Mom is satisfied they are pretty up-tight about home, she does another interesting thing. She puts her wing over the nest and she says something audible to the eaglets.

If we could understand eagle talk, she probably said, "Get off the briars and onto my wing."

These two baby eagles scramble up onto their mother's wing. Here they are in a great, soft place again. They nestle down into their mother's feathers, loving every minute of it.

Without any warning, Mom dives out of the nest. These eaglets grab onto her feathers for dear life. She flies out over the countryside giving them a marvelous ride. They start to get some confidence and look down.

"Boy, isn't this great? Look at that!"

As they are flying over the countryside, Mom starts to circle upward. She goes higher and higher, getting way up in the sky. The eaglets are loving it. Suddenly, without any warning whatsoever, Mom turns upside down and shakes the baby eagles off her back. These two eaglets come screaming out of the sky. They don't know how to fly yet and they tumble head over wing screaming bloody murder. Then Mom does what the naturalists refer to as a miracle of nature; she swoops down and catches them before they hit the ground.

Now, if you saw the movie *Superman*, you know that it is possible. The mother eagle swoops down and catches her babies. They are wide-eyed. But what does Mom do? She starts to circle back up. They know what is coming up this time and they are hanging on for dear life. She gets up high again and does the same maneuver shaking the eaglets off her back. They come screaming out of the sky the second time. Once again Mom swoops down.

About the third time these eaglets are screaming out of the sky and they see Mom swoop by with her magnificent wings, they say to themselves, "You know, we have two of those feathered things. Why don't we use them?"

And, for the first time, those new wings come out

and the eagles fly. They are off on their own. They never come home, ever again. They have been taught well. They are old enough to leave, and before long they will make their own nests and teach their young as their mother has taught them.

In a very real sense, that is what happens to us. We get dropped until we discover our wings. And a lot of us come screaming out of the sky just like those baby eagles. We see great men and women around us who have the wings of faith and courage and all those other necessary skills to make it in this world. Finally we begin to say, "You know, I think I can do that too. Why don't I try?" And then, on one of these trips out of the sky, we find ourselves putting the wings out, and we are flying, too—just like those eagles.

The Eagle and the Chickens

The second story builds upon the first. It is a story of a naturalist who was walking by a farm on one occasion. He looked into the chicken coop, and there amongst the chickens was a large eagle.

He learned that the farmer had found a giant egg and put it in with the chicken eggs for them to hatch. When the farmer discovered the eaglet, he thought it was a funny-looking chicken and left it with the chickens to raise.

The naturalist went to the farmer and said, "You know you have an eagle out there with your chickens?"

"I don't have any eagles, just chickens," replied the farmer.

"Come here and I'll show you that you have an eagle out there." The naturalist takes the farmer to where the eagle is and says, "That is an eagle."

"Nope. It's just a chicken."

"I know what an eagle looks like. Have you ever

seen a chicken with a six-foot wing span? That is an eagle."

"It's a chicken."

"I'll prove to you that it is an eagle."

The naturalist took the eagle and put it up on a fencepost. He pointed the eagle's head towards the sun and whispered in its ear, "You're an eagle. Fly!"

The eagle looked up at the sky and then back at the chickens. It hopped down from the fencepost and back with the chickens.

The farmer was quick to reply, "See, I told you it was a chicken."

The naturalist shook his head and said, "No, it's an eagle. Tomorrow I will prove it to you."

The next day the naturalist was back bright and early. He took the eagle up to the weather vane on top of the barn. He said to the eagle, "You are an eagle. Fly!" Again he pointed the eagle's head toward the sun. Again the eagle looked at the sky and then back at the chickens. It hopped down from the barn into the chicken pen.

The farmer just shook his head.

"It is an eagle. Tomorrow I will prove it to you," and the naturalist left.

The following day the naturalist was back early and took the farmer and the eagle to a high mountain where the eagle couldn't see the barnyard anymore. He put the eagle out on the edge of a cliff. He pointed its head at the sun and said, "You are an eagle. Fly!"

This old eagle looked up at the sun—he couldn't see the barnyard anymore—and spread its wings and flew. It flew out over the countryside and never came back.

The naturalist looked at the farmer and said, *"That is an eagle."*

I share that story with you because everyone of you

was born an eagle. Unfortunately, many of us have been raised in the chicken coop. I'm not talking about your homes—please don't be offended by that. But we have been raised to believe that we are chickens. We live like chickens because we grew up with chickens. You think, "Everybody around me is a chicken; therefore, I'd better be a chicken. I don't want to be an eagle and embarrass anybody."

Perspective 1: I am a child of God.

The first perspective from which I want you to look at yourself is: You are an eagle. You came to this earth with an eternal heritage as a son or daughter of God. The potential for greatness is there. Remember that. Don't forget it. When you look at yourself in the mirror see yourself as an eagle, a child of God.

Perspective 2: I am here at this time in history because of who I am.

I will take you through a timeline of events to build a case for who I believe you are. I want you to ask yourself as you read through this, "Why am I here today?"

The year zero on our timeline starts with the Savior's birth. The Savior began his ministry in the year 30 A.D. He created a church, selected apostles and leaders, and organized a physical organization. Three years later, because the people didn't like this organization or what he was teaching, he was rejected. The classic form of rejection in those days was crucifixion, so he was crucified.

The ministry of the apostles was between the year 33 A.D. and 96 A.D. They traveled throughout the world to build up the church. Within those sixty years, the apostles were all killed, save John the Revelator.

They were killed in some extremely wicked ways. Peter, for example, died in Rome. Peter was crucified and he didn't feel worthy to be crucified the same way the Savior was, so he asked to be nailed to the cross with his feet up and his head down. His enemies willingly accommodated him and crucified him upside down. All of the apostles died in similar cruel, brutal, and ugly ways.

In 96 A.D., John the Revelator was banished to the Isle of Patmos where he wrote the *Book of Revelations*. There is no more knowledge of John recorded until the restoration of the gospel.

Between 96 A.D. and 320 A.D., what was the plight of the Christians? What happened to the Christians during this time period? History reveals that they were not very popular for most of that time. To survive they went underground in Rome. You have heard about the catacombs and the Christians being fodder for the lions and gladiators.

After a hundred-year period, new philosophies and concepts began to take hold. In the year 325 A.D. a man by the name of Constantine decided to have a meeting. He called some of the brilliant scholars of his time together. Constantine was the emperor, a very powerful man. He had some unique challenges in bringing his nation together. He called wise men and sent them to a place called Nicaea.

He told them, "I want you to go there and have a meeting. I want you to come back and tell me what God is like. Nobody can really tell me what God is like, and I've got to know. And when you come back and tell me, that is the way everybody is going to believe in God. You understand?" He was the emperor. You bet they did!

The wise men went to Nicea for a meeting which lasted several weeks. At the end of the meeting, they came back with a statement on God, which has become known as the Nicene Creed. How many of you have read the Nicene Creed? I really encourage you all to read it. What it says in essence is that God, Christ and the Holy Ghost are all the same person. Not really a person of flesh and bone and blood, not really the same but sort of the same—a very confusing definition. That is the basic message of the creed.

During this time we find the formal beginnings of the Catholic Church. We also find the beginnings of the era of the reign of the popes. This was a bloody period of history. In 785 A.D., there was a second Nicene Council held under the Empress Irene. In this council it was determined that they would canonize saints. The worship of idols came into the religion.

Somewhere between 785 to 900 A.D., there was a woman pope. This isn't taught anywhere in the writings of the Catholic Church but there is documented proof. There was also one era, 1100 A.D., when there were three popes, each believing that he was the only true and living pope, and warring one with another to prove who was the legitimate pope.

The reign of the popes was not a religiously tolerant period of time. More people were killed in the name of Christianity between 320 A.D. and the late 1800s than in all of our wars put together. In 1200 A.D. there was an interesting pope by the name of Innocent III. The reason he was significant is that he was known as the Boss Pope. He had several wars he was trying to finance. A very powerful emperor, king, and pope all wrapped up into one. Because he was having difficulty in financing his wars, he introduced into the church a principle called the sale of indulgences.

This is a unique program where one can pay for the remission of his sins. In other words, we go out and have a great time on Saturday; and on Sunday we come in, confess our sins, pay x number of dollars, and our sins are gone. In fact, in later years one could even pre-pay for sins. Pope Innocent III raised large amounts of money for his wars.

The reason this principle is significant historically is because of what happened 300 years later. The invention and appearance of the printing press occurred in 1450 A.D. You need to know that between the time of Christ and 1500 A.D. very few people knew how to read. In fact, it was considered a sin to read. There are some parts of the world where as late as 1957 Catholics were not allowed to read the scriptures. In 1500 A.D. a revolution took place in Europe. Not a revolution of war, steel, and that sort of thing, but a different kind of revolution. What was it? The Renaissance. The Renaissance was an age of enlightenment, a cultural revolution. People for the first time started to read because there was material available as a result of the printing press. Things they had never read before enlightened them. People began to question things they had never questioned before.

What American doesn't know what happened in 1492? You better know that. Columbus showed up. He was a product of the Renaissance. He conned somebody into giving him three boats and then disappeared. Months later he returned bringing news of a new world.

Another product of the Renaissance appeared on the horizon in 1517. He was named Martin Luther. He was a Catholic priest—not a rabble-rouser, not one trying to destroy the church, but a faithful Augustinian monk. Because of the Renaissance and the ability now to read ancient scripture, he went back and read some of the original documents. The principle which bothered him the most was the sale of indulgences.

He said, "I can't find anywhere in the ancient

writings that says anything about the sale of indulgences. I don't think that's right." So he developed
ninety-five questions which he wanted answered by the
church. He nailed these questions to the church at Wit-
tenburg, Germany. After several weeks (word didn't get
around all that fast at that time in history), people
would wander by the church and say, "There's
something from Martin Luther, whoever he is."

In time these questions of Luther caused a terrific
furor in Europe. Because of these questions, Luther was
called before several courts of the Catholic Church.
They told him, "Luther, you've got to stop this. No more
questions. You'd better stop it or you're going to be in
big trouble."

Luther replied, "I'm not trying to destroy the
church; all I want is answers to my questions."

The church would not answer because there were
no answers to his questions. In 1521 he was excom-
municated from the church. The Catholic Church,
because it had the right and power to do it, issued a
proclamation which said, "It would not be considered
murder to kill Martin Luther." In fact, one would be
doing the church a favor if he would do away with him.

This is a classic form of rejection. Martin Luther
had to go underground. A number of people believed
what he was saying. They approached him—wealthy
people of Germany—and said, "Will you head up a
church? We think you are right."

For a long time Luther said, "No. I don't want to
head up a church; that's not why I'm doing this. I love
the Catholic Church."

But when the church started trying to kill him, he
changed his mind He reluctantly accepted the role as
the first leader of what is now the Lutheran Church.
Never did he claim any revelation; never did he say,
"Thus sayeth the Lord, because I've talked to him."

What he did say was, "I've got some questions; things don't seem to be right." With Martin Luther began a major period in European history that we know as the Reformation.

In 1534, a little farther down the time line, Henry VIII, over in England, was having some marriage trouble. Remember Henry VIII? He was an interesting guy. He wanted to get rid of his wife. He went to the pope and asked permission to divorce her.

The pope said, "That's not part of the program, Henry VIII."

"Well, I'll tell you what. Luther's doing okay outside of the church; I'm going to do it too." Henry VIII broke with the Catholic Church and created the Church of England. What is the Church of England in America today? The Episcopal Church. For its beginnings it had no revelation, no formal experience with God—just a great way to solve a marriage problem.

We have another reformer surface in 1540 by the name of John Calvin. He comes on the scene in the Switzerland and France area. He says, "You know, I think Luther is right. There are a lot of things I don't buy of his, but I think he is on the right track." Calvin started the Huguenot program.

Who are the Huguenots in America today? They are the Presbyterians. In 1560 another John, John Knox over in England, comes onto the scene. He is a disciple of Calvin and Luther. He says, "Those guys are great; I don't agree with everything they're saying, but they are on the right track." John Knox started the Puritan movement of the Great Reformers.

To illustrate the atmosphere in which the reformers were laboring in 1572, an experience occurred in Paris, on Saint Bartholomew's Day, when the Catholics rose up and slaughtered thousands of Protestants and Reformers. They said in essence, "You know, we've had enough of this stuff. We don't want to hear about this reforming junk anymore." They slaughtered them in the streets. That act reflected the flavor of the Reformation. It was not an isolated incident. Because of the violent attitude, what happened in 1620, just forty-eight years after Saint Bartholomew's Day? The Puritans boarded their boats and said, "We've had it with this stuff here! We are going to this place Columbus found where we can believe the way we want to believe." So they left and sailed to America.

Were the Puritans a religiously tolerant group? No. But they understood that if they wanted freedom of religion they must allow it for everyone else.

Between 1620 and 1776, we find the birth of a magnificent nation. In 1776 the Founding Fathers wrote to King George telling him to take his army home to England. They had had enough. No more taxes. They wanted to be on their own. King George was not very excited about the letter. It was the Declaration of Independence. A war started that lasted five years: the American Revolution. By some miracle—if you study the Revolutionary War, you will find it is a very real miracle—we won. We beat the British, which we weren't supposed to do. A new nation was born.

Who was born in 1805? That's right, Joseph Smith. A future prophet of God.

What happened in 1812? The War of 1812 took place. It was significant because we beat the British soundly this time. They said at the beginning of the War of 1812, "You know, you embarrassed us a few years ago, and we don't like to be embarrassed." So they sailed up the Potomac River in their ships, shelled the White House, and burned it to the ground. But this war we had a navy, we had our own ships. The USS Constitution was commissioned in 1797; a beautiful ship. We also had an army. We beat the British handily. We said to the world, "Don't mess with us anymore." We had written what was then and is today (if we'd stop messing with it) a divine document, the United States Constitution, which guarantees the freedom of religion.

What happened in 1820? The first vision. God and Jesus Christ appeared to the young boy prophet, Joseph Smith. What the Lord had to do, through inspiration, was prepare a people that could withstand a visitation from Him. Suppose that Joseph Smith had arrived back in 1100 A.D. and said to the world, "You know what? I just talked with God and Jesus Christ. Do you want to know what they had to say?

What would have happened to Joseph Smith? He would have been killed so fast he wouldn't have been able to repeat his question twice. But by 1820 the Lord had prepared a nation, and He didn't wait very long to reveal His message. I think the Lord was pretty excited about the whole turn of events. He couldn't wait to get Joseph Smith down here.

What happened in 1830? The Church was organized and officially became The Church of Jesus Christ of Latter-day Saints.

Do you know what else happened in 1830 in Washington D.C.? The United States Congress closed the U.S. Patent Office. In the *Congressional Record* you can read in 1830, "We are closing the United States Patent Office because, in our opinion, everything has been invented that could possibly be invented." Isn't that interesting? I want you to know they have reopened it since then.

Why has there been so much progress since 1830? Did it happen just by chance? In the brief one hundred and fifty years, more has happened than in the previous nineteen hundred. Incredible progress has been made in every field from medicine to data processing. Why? I believe it is because revelation is back.

The Lord is once again speaking to his prophets on the earth.

Do you know what significant event happened in 1818, just a few years before the restoration? Are you aware who was born in 1818? Karl Marx. Isn't that interesting? The opposition. Heavy opposition. Who is winning statistically today? Karl Marx, although the political climate is changing daily.

I want you now to ask yourself the question as you look back over this time line: Why me, now? Why was I born when I was born? Why wasn't I born in Russia in 933 A.D.? Have you really asked yourself that question? I want to tell you: you were born *now* because you were somebody in the pre-existence.

I Am a General

On one occasion in Salt Lake City, many years ago, a man, not a General Authority, was speaking at a fireside to young adults. David O. McKay, the president of the Church, was sitting in the audience. That would be an interesting experience to talk with the prophet sitting in the audience. You would want to make sure you were straight with what you said. The speaker got carried away with the Spirit and proceeded to say the following:

"I'm inspired to tell you tonight, young people, that in the pre-existence you served as captains and generals in the war in heaven."

Then the speaker went on with his talk. As he finished he started to get very nervous and thought, "Boy oh boy, here's President McKay sitting here. What have I done?" At the end of the meeting he approached President McKay and said, "Look, I got a little carried away up here tonight; I'm embarrassed. Was I out in left field? Did I make a mistake tonight?"

President McKay looked at him and said, "Actually you did. There were not any captains here tonight, only generals."

Joseph Smith, on one occasion said, "If I were to tell you who I really am, you would slay me for blasphemy." Did you know he said that? Yes, he knew who he really was.

I want you to look at yourself through these two perspectives. First, you are a child of God; and second, you are here at this point in time in the history of the world because of who you are and what you were before you came to this earth. Don't forget it. Act with that knowledge and you won't disappoint yourself. You will realize your full potential.

I act with confidence because I know the qualities of my eternal heritage and I act with those qualities. I am an eagle. I act as an eagle.

HEADWATERS

Paying attention to the cues from our eternal heritage is a key to self-discovery.

Personal success comes as we improve our ability to listen to signals. They are sent to help us avoid problems, do what is right, and achieve our greatest potential. One such cue is the promptings of the Spirit. The following story illustrates what happens when we listen to the Spirit.

The Spirit Whispered, "Cheat!"

A man, who was not a member of the Church, but whose wife and family had been attending church for a number of years, particularly enjoyed going to the father-and-son outings. He was large in stature, a gruff outdoorsman; and he smoked a big, long cigar. Because of his personality, word went throughout the ward that no one was to pressure Brother So-and-so into joining the Church. "He's active like he is, so don't bug him."

Therefore, nobody ever bothered talking to him about the Church. A new family moved into the ward and this message had not yet reached the father of this family. Both fathers were at a father-and-son outing. They were sitting around the fire when Brother So-and-so pulled out his cigar, an unusual happening at a Church father-and-son outing. The fellow who was new to the ward looked through the fire and said, "Aren't you a member of the Church?"

"No. I'm not a member of the Church."

"But I see you in church all the time."

"That's right. I go to church with my family. I enjoy it."

And then this good brother, because he didn't know any better, opened his mouth and said, "Why don't you join the Church?"

Everybody else around the fire froze in place. One could almost hear the thought racing through their minds, "You're not supposed to ask this brother that question."

Still holding his cigar, he looked down and said, "Well, nobody has ever asked me before."

And the member said, "Well, I'm asking you. Why don't you join the Church? Your wife is a member, your children are members; why don't you join?" He paused for a moment and then continued, "Will you join the Church?" The air went blue around the fire.

Brother So-and-so looked up, all the while puffing on his cigar. Everybody else was as nervous as they could be. Brother So-and-so was sort of a kidder, so he stood up and said, "I'll tell you what. I have a quarter here. I'll flip this quarter and if it comes up heads I will join the Church; if it comes up tails, I won't join the Church. How 'bout that?"

This good brother, being a new member of the ward, didn't have anything to lose so he said, "Great. Flip your quarter." The nonmember put his cigar out and flipped his quarter. The quarter sailed through the air; he caught it and put it on his arm. When he lifted his hand to see the result, it was tails and he was not to join the Church.

As he stood there in the light of the campfire the Spirit spoke to him for the first time. It was almost audible. The voice whispered very clearly in his ear, "Cheat!" He took the quarter off his arm, and put it back in his pocket, and said, "It was heads. I guess I'll have to join the Church." The next day the font was filled and that good brother was baptized.

An interesting chain of events occurred in this story. The member who didn't know any better opened his mouth. And another brother responded to a prompting that he had been putting off for a long time. As a result, he became a great member of that ward. Why? Because he chose to listen to the Spirit. Normally the Spirit will not tell you to cheat, but on this particular occasion it did and it was right. How can we develop the ability, the spiritual maturity, to identify and then respond to the promptings of the Spirit? Let me give you a little saying; I want you to commit it to memory. I would like you to make this a part of you and never forget it.

What we do depends upon how we feel about what we know.

Lloyd Davis

Whether or not you do anything with what you read or hear depends upon the feelings you generate about that knowledge.

Here is another true story.

Tragedy in Tasmania

In Australia some time ago, a very large oil tanker was steaming up the river into the harbor at Tasmania. The city is built on both sides of the river. To enable people to get from one side of the city to the other a very high bridge was built across the river. It was not a draw bridge. The roadway was one hundred and fifty feet above the water so that tankers could make their way underneath it without having to lift the bridge.

This particular night it was rainy, dark, and windy. The oil tanker was a little off course and as a result, it ran into the stanchion that supported the bridge. Because of the size of the tanker and the power with which it hit the bridge, a one hundred foot section crumbled and fell. It draped itself over the bow of the boat.

There were cars on the section of the bridge that fell; two or three cars followed close behind, did not see the road disappear, and drove off the end into the river. A fourth car, seeing what had happened, was able to stop just before it came to the edge of the tragic precipice. A man jumped out of his car, went to the edge of the bridge, and saw the tanker floundering in the water. He understood what had happened and realized in that instant his responsibility to the rest of the oncoming traffic.

He had to warn them. He barked some quick instructions to his wife to run the car around to aim the headlights the other way and he would run down the street to stop the traffic. He ran frantically, waving his arms, from the side of the road.

Remember the last time you were driving down a highway at night during a rain storm and somebody was on the side of the road waving his arms. How did you react? You probably said, "Sorry, Jack, I'm in a hurry. Somebody else will take care of you," and you went right on by them. That is exactly what happened with the first three cars to pass him. They saw a wild man waving his arms and said, "It's raining. I'm not picking up any screwball tonight." They drove off into the night and off the end of the bridge. The fourth car came and by this time the man was frantic. He threw himself into the street so that the car either had to stop or run over him. The car screeched to a stop and the man in the street quickly pointed out what was now a very dangerous situation. The feelings the driver had about the fellow in the street now changed dramatically. Instead of being upset for being stopped, he was pretty grateful. He now helped stop other cars. Traffic backed up and when the drivers went to the edge of the bridge, they saw the awful tragedy down below.

Snakes and Alligators

In a very real sense, the Savior is standing on the highway of our lives. To most people he appears as an ordinary fellow. He is waving his arms to call our attention to the road we are on. He is warning us, "This is a painful road. If you just stop and listen to me for a moment, I will tell you about a better way. If you find the better way, you will not have to go through what you are about to face on this road."

The interesting thing is, many of us, knowing the man and having heard his message, go driving by. It is like walking through the jungle and suddenly there is a great pit filled with snakes and alligators and we have to get across it. We have the option of going down through the snakes and alligators, or crawling across a tree trunk that has fallen to avoid what is at the bottom of the pit. Anyone in his right mind would say, "I don't want anything to do with those snakes and alligators," and would go across the tree trunk. Without recognizing the consequences, some of us not only select the pit but dive into it. We say, "I'd like to see what those snakes and alligators are like, and we dive in. Then, when we are walking across the bottom of the pit with snakes and alligators hanging all over us, we say, "You know, this isn't as neat as I thought it was going to be."

We look up at the tree trunk going across the hole

and say, "Boy, I was really dumb. Why did I jump in here? Why didn't I go across at the top?"

When we get to the other side we start climbing up. Some of us make it. Some die in the pit.

But those of us who crawl up the other side are sore; we suffer pain and have sorrow. We sit there repenting of our foolish choice. Still aching with pain we say, "If only I had gone across the tree." We then develop some very strong feelings about others preparing to climb down on the other side. We call out to them, "Hey, the tree's really the better way, guys. Take the tree."

If we desire to develop an ability to listen to that Spirit (which is all around us and will help direct us in a very real, practical way, in our business ventures, in our families, in our avocations, in our community efforts, in every decision), we must recognize that the Spirit is there.

But before that Spirit can work, we must learn to identify it; we have to acquire some spiritual maturity. We must know who we are. If we know who we are and feel good about who we are, then we will be able to meet every problem and receive the revelation which is our right to have.

But how do we develop spiritual maturity? We must develop a power called faith—faith in God and faith in ourselves. Knowing that we can do what we *will* today. How is faith developed? Faith is developed by mastering celestial habits.

The Missionary: Before and After

The missionary has an interesting experience in the Church called a missionary farewell. Have you ever been to a missionary farewell? In that meeting, the ward doesn't sit the way it normally does. The Primary,

Seminary, and Sunday School teachers who had anything to do with the missionary who is leaving all sit on the first three rows. During the prelude music a very interesting conversation is taking place.

A Primary teacher will turn to a Sunday School teacher and say, "Can you believe this? John is going on a mission."

"No, I can't believe it. That's why I'm sitting on the front row. Look at him. He's got ears. I haven't seen his ears for years."

The meeting starts. Mom gets up, and—moms are like this at farewells—she carries on forever. She has the right to. She has gone through blood, sweat, and tears for her boy. By the time she is through, John has only four minutes at the end; so he bears a nervous testimony. He then disappears for two years.

In another two years, we have another meeting in the Church called a missionary homecoming. Have you ever been to one of these? The same people sit on the first three rows, engaging in the same conversation, "Can you believe this? The gospel must be true after all. Look at John."

Instead of the red in his cheeks, he has little lines at the edges of his eyes; and his hair isn't as full as it used to be. He has a little different look about him. He's changed. He has become different. Instead of a four-minute nervous testimony, this time he preaches for forty minutes. The bishop has to ask him to sit down because another ward needs to come in.

We go away from that experience and say, "Isn't that neat what the mission has done for John? Wow! He sure has changed!"

Disciplines of Change

Do you know what brought the change in the

missionary? Two basic disciplines. He discovered when he got into the mission field that just because he was captain of the football team at home didn't make any difference. The fact that the cheerleaders had adored him and sighed over him didn't make any difference. If he was going to succeed in this mission experience, he needed the Spirit. He must learn to identify that Spirit and listen to it. So he mastered two disciplines. *He studied the scriptures every day,* as he had never done before, and *he prayed every day* as he had never done before. Do you know how many times a missionary and his companion will pray together in a day? Seven to eight times, on their knees, a minimum. Ask yourself, you returned missionaries, how often did you kneel yesterday? Or the day before?

At the end of each one of my missionaries' missions (I had over six hundred missionaries in my mission), I had the sweet experience of interviewing each one. As I sat with them, I would commit them to continue to study the scriptures every day. We have hundreds of church books and they are great, but they are not the headwaters; they are downstream. The headwaters are the scriptures, the words of Christ. I would commit my missionaries to read these scriptures.

They would say, "You bet, President Smith. I'll do it."

I would also commit them to say their prayers every day and as often as they did in the mission field. The reaction to these commitments were always the same. They were dumbfounded that I would even ask them such questions.

"Well, President Smith, that's easy. Of course I'm going to do that."

"Are you going to do it, Elder?"

"Yes, I'll do it."

Two or three times I would get them to say, "Yes, I'll do it."

Then they would come home. The homecoming is over. What happens next? I hear missionaries saying, "Boy, I miss the spirit of the mission field." When I hear that statement a great big red flag goes up in my mind. I say, "Why? Why, Elder, do you miss the spirit from the mission field?"

"Well, I don't know."

"Are you studying the scriptures?"

"Sort of."?

Do you know what the Mormon definition of *sort of* is? It means, "I haven't touched my scriptures for months."

I ask the missionary this next question, "Are you praying often? Every day?"

"Well, yeah."

"How many times yesterday?"

"Let me see. Yeah, before I went to bed last night."

Like so many, off goes the spiritual spigot. It is just like turning off a hose. We get used to the flow of the Spirit and then we come home. Instead of five, six, and eight times on our knees, it's once quickly before we go to bed at night, if it's not too cold.

Instead of studying the scriptures two hours every day, it is twenty minutes before priesthood meeting, if we have to teach a class. But we carry them because it makes us look good. Everybody thinks we study them. Of course, they are all marked up because we marked them in the mission field. But we haven't marked anything since we got home. We open them up and everybody says, "Wow! Look how he marked his scriptures."

We stop doing and the Spirit stops communicating. Then we lose that critical tie with the Spirit.

I've talked with a number of my missionaries who have had trouble since they have returned home. Invariably, the questions were not answered well on those two issues. It has something to do with this poem.

HABIT

I am your constant companion.
I am your greatest helper or your heaviest
burden.
I will push you onward or drag you down
to failure.
I am completely at your command.
Half the things you do, you might just
as well turn over to me,
And I will be able to do them quickly and
correctly.
I am easily managed; you must merely
be firm with me.
Show me exactly how you want
something done,
And after a few lessons I will do it
automatically.
I am the servant of all great men
And, alas, of all failures as well.
Those who are great, I have made great.
Those who are failures, I have made
failures.
I am not a machine, though I work with
all the precision of a machine
Plus the intelligence of a man.
You may run me for profit, or run me for
ruin;
It makes no difference to me.
Take me, train me, be firm with me
And I will put the world at your feet.
Be easy with me, and I will destroy you.
Who am I?
I am HABIT!

author unknown

The celestial habits that save, that give us the ability to listen, to identify, and respond to the promptings of the Holy Spirit, come from some very basic disciplines—disciplines we have heard about all our lives. Often we say, "I know that stuff already," and we back away.

My young people, the Lord has you here today because he needs a people of great faith. We are facing a time in this great country economically and, in the world, politically where you had better have a testimony of your own, or you are not going to make it. It is that simple.

Going Home: Faith Works, Doesn't It?

When we had been in the mission field just a few days we didn't have any furniture in our office as yet because we had just opened a new mission. We didn't even have a telephone, so we had to use the pay telephone in the hall. We stationed one of our missionaries in the hall to listen for the phone. The other tenants in the building always wondered why this suited guy was sitting out by the phone.

During one of these first days, a call came from one of the missionaries. Our lookout came into my office and said, "President Smith, there is an elder on the phone. He sounds upset." I went to the phone.

A voice said, "President Smith, you don't know me yet and I really don't know you either. I have a serious problem at home. I must leave immediately."

I asked him, "May we talk about this here at the office?"

"Yes, maybe we'd better. It's important that I talk to you, because it's important that I go home right away."

He had about a half hour drive to make it to the

mission home, and I started to think to myself, "What am I going to say to this young man? I've been here three days. I am supposed to save all my missionaries." I had made a commitment while going through the Missionary Training Center experience for mission presidents that I wasn't going to lose any of *my missionaries*. I heard that missionaries fall away but I wasn't going to lose any. Well, I matured during my three years as mission president. We lost more missionaries than I like to think about.

The elder arrived and proceeded to tell me the following story. He said, "President Smith, I'm a convert to the Church. I've been a member for three years. I have been in the mission field eighteen months. My father is not a member of the Church and is a severe alcoholic. My mother is not a member of the Church. My brother who is fourteen, large in stature for his age, is having a very serious drug problem. He beats my mother regularly. My father beats my mother regularly. In the last eighteen months, my mother has called me every three or four days and begged me to come home. It used to be my role at home to protect my mother from my father and brother."

He went on, "I just got a call last night from my mother. My father came home drunk, had lost all their money again, and had severely beaten my mother. My brother had participated in the beating. My mother is badly bruised and injured. She said that she had purchased a weapon. If I do not come home tomorrow, she is going to kill herself. She is going to commit suicide." He finished, "I really think I ought to go."

As I sat there and listened to this story, I thought to myself, "Boy, if I ever heard a good reason for going home from a mission, I've just heard it." I found myself wanting to say, "Elder, I'll take you to the airport myself. I'll buy your ticket. I'll get you a Lear Jet and fly you home personally, if I have to. We will get you home now!"

When he finished telling me his story, and it was my turn to talk, I couldn't believe what I was hearing myself say. I said to him, "Elder, I don't suppose I have ever heard a more practical, real opportunity to exercise faith than what I have heard just now. Do you suppose the Lord wants you to finish your mission?"

"Yes, I'm sure of that."

"How about President Kimball?"

"Yes, he does, too."

"Your bishop, stake president?"

"Yes."

"How about your mission president?"

"Yes, I'm sure you do."

"How about you, Elder? Do you want to finish your mission?"

"President Smith, I'd love to be able to finish my mission, but I can't." Tears came to his eyes.

I said, "Do you suppose if you put this in the hands of the Lord that He could take care of it?"

I just sat there and looked at him for awhile. After a minute of silence I continued, "I'll go and call your mother and just see how things are."

I went to our pay phone and called his mother who was in Florida. I got a very distraught woman on the phone. She said something like this, "Mr. Smith, I don't know who you are and I don't know anything about this Mormon mission thing, but I'm telling you now if my son isn't home tomorrow I'm going to kill myself. I have purchased a weapon." She described a large-caliber hand gun. "I'm going to do it; I can't take it anymore." And then she hung up.

Well, I had a long walk from that telephone back to my office. All my other feelings came back, "Get him home, President Smith, just get him home." So I went back to the office and looked at him. He was sitting there with a very intense look on his face.

I said, "Elder, what do you think? Can the Lord take care of this thing? Is faith real?"

We just sat there in silence for a long time, and then he looked at me and said, "President Smith, if you tell me my mom will be okay, I'll stay."

I remember I took a big breath, looked him in the eye, and said, "Elder, she'll be okay."

He said, "I'll stay."

He got up, shook my hand and left. Suddenly I was very alone.

I went home that night and spent a wakeful night. I remember praying as I think I've never prayed before, and I've done some real pleading with the Lord in my life. I found myself getting a little short with Him. "Did you hear what I said today, Lord? Did you hear what I promised this kid in your name today? You'd better back me up, Lord." I don't usually talk to the Lord like that, but I was scared.

The next day I went back to the office. Every time that phone rang I could hear somebody telling me that there had been a death in Florida. My faith wasn't all that strong. But the phone call never came; and somehow, through a very real miracle, things got better. Well, that elder finally went home. On his release day he came to my office. He sat down and we just looked at each other for a few minutes. Sweet experience. Have you ever had one of those experiences where the Spirit is so thick there isn't anything right to say? We just sat there basking in this feeling. I finally looked at him and said, "Elder, faith works, doesn't it?"

He said, "Yes, it works. I have a testimony of that."

We hugged each other, and he left. There was a powerful young man who discovered the real power of faith.

I want to bear my testimony to you that faith is no joke. It is real. Mountains get moved by faith. It is by faith you can know who you are. It is by faith that you can discover what you can be—an eagle, not a chicken. I have a testimony of faith and who you are. I hope you have that same vision. If you can get that vision and realize who you are, things will occur in your life that others will refer to as miracles, but you'll know it is because you've mastered the principle of faith.

I am better prepared to say no to temptations because I am paying attention to the signals coming from the Spirit.

PUNGIE STICKS

**Unwavering obedience to the true principles
we learn will assure us spiritual survival.**

There probably is not a more critical concept or principle of the gospel that we have to deal with now as young people than the principle of obedience. The reason we go to meetings is to learn how to identify the hazards and problems that face us in the world. The reason we go to Seminary is to learn to recognize the pitfalls that are out there and then try to avoid them. The reason we go to Sunday School, the reason we go through the Primary program, and to sacrament meeting, and all the meetings we go to is for training experiences. These training experiences are vital to our survival.

Vietnam: Training Experience

When I returned home from my mission, I was drafted into the army. I had a close friend who was drafted into the army about the same time. He went into the infantry. I went into the artillery—because the artillery rides and the infantry walks. This was in 1965 when the Vietnam War was getting hot and heavy. Because of Vietnam much of the training we experienced was to teach us how to stay alive in combat. The Vietnam war continued to escalate and a lot of our young men were sent there. Many of them were dying so the training was geared specifically to teach us to stay alive in Vietnam.

As I sat through that training, I began to discover some of the devices that the Vietcong had developed to either kill or maim our men.

I would like to share a couple of those with you and tell you about the training. One of the devices that the Vietnamese developed was a thing called a pungie stick. How many of you know what a pungie stick is? A pungie stick is a young bamboo rod about as big around as my little finger. They sharpen this bamboo rod to a very sharp razor point. Then they take it and soak it in human urine for three days. Because the bamboo is very young, it absorbs all the poison. There is nothing more poisonous than that after it stands.

The Vietnamese then go along the trails where they know the American GI is going to be walking. They dig pits along both sides of the trail every twelve or fifteen feet. These pits are just a little bigger than a man and about three to four feet deep. After they have finished digging these pits, they fill the bottom with pungie sticks. These sticks are imbedded in the mud with the point coming straight up from the mud. The tops of these pits are meticulously covered so that the GI cannot tell that the ground has ever been disturbed.

The reason they do this is that they know that the American GI, when he is walking down a trail and hears somebody shooting at him, will dive off the trail for cover. It was the GI's first instinct, a carry-over from the Second World War training.

So, when we first went to Vietnam, quite a number of our soldiers died in those pits. They would dive off the trail. Sometimes the Vietcong would just shoot in the air. Our men would get scared and jump off the trail and land in those pits. It is an ugly way to die.

After awhile the GI's decided to jump off the trail

feet first. Those sticks were so sharp they would go right through the boots. Some of the sticks would go up into the calf. The American Army put metal plates in the bottom of all the GI's shoes that went to Vietnam so the pungie stick could not puncture the boot.

They then decided they had better teach our guys to recognize those pits, so a great deal of the training was to recognize, as we walked along a trail, the pungie stick pits.

Another little device that they developed with pungie sticks was to take a board about as big as a book, and stick about twenty of these things through the front of the board. Then the Vietnamese would pull that board back into the bushes mounted on a large bamboo spring. Next, they would stick a small piano wire across the trail that was attached to the board. If you were walking down the trail and missed seeing that wire and hit it, you would hear the brief rushing sound of the pungie stick board coming straight at you. If you heard the sound, it was too late. There isn't anybody alive fast enough to get out of the way. That board would come across the trail at eighty miles an hour. We had many of our guys who missed seeing the wire end up with one of those boards attached to his chest. Another ugly way to die.

The Vietnamese also developed a little mine about the size of a tuna can. That mine was made not to kill but to maim. They knew that if they could blow off a foot or a leg, it would take three or four other GI's to get him back to help. But if they killed him, the Americans would leave him there and the rest would keep on going in the assault. Once the Vietnamese learned which way our guys were coming, they would drop these little tuna cans all over the place. When our guys would go marching through the fields, and you would hear these small explosions, our guys would be

losing their feet and their arms. Our leaders decided
that we had better learn to recognize those little tuna
fish cans too.

There was a device, a bigger mine, which the Vietnamese developed. It was set in the middle of the road.
It had a pressure plate on its top. The pressure plate
was the only thing that showed. They would cover it
with dust so you could hardly see it. This mine was
designed to blow the front end off a vehicle. So when
our trucks would travel down a trail or path and hit
one of these mines, it would blow off the front end of
the truck. The way we identified those mines was to
take one of our GI's and sit him on the front bumper
of the truck. It was his job to spot the mines.

Do you suppose he was motivated to find those
mines? You better believe he was, because if he missed
it, what would happen? He would go up with the front
end of that truck. Part of our training was to help us
identify those mines.

Another mine was designed by the enemy to kill,
not just maim. It would level an area about the size of
a chapel. It was sunk in the ground and the only thing
that came up out of the ground were three wires. Those
three wires were just a short distance above the ground
and would usually be hidden in the grass. If you tripped one of those wires, it would level you and
everything within a twenty-yard radius. So the army
decided that we'd better learn how to identify those
three little wires. A great deal of the training was spent
learning to watch for those mines. As I went through
basic training, I was taught how to recognize all of these
hazards.

The interesting thing I found, as I sat in the warmth
of Fort Polk, Louisiana, witnessing this training and
looking around the classroom, was the number of guys
who were asleep. How many do you suppose were

asleep? About half—half of them were sleeping. This bothered the instructors of the school so they decided to bring some realism into our training. They brought vivid color pictures back from Vietnam of people who had died in the pits or had been blown up by the mines. They would flash these colored pictures up on the screen. That woke up about a third more of the class. But we still had quite a few that would continue to sleep.

After the classroom, our instructors would have us go down trails in real-life situations. I'll never forget the day I was going down a trail. These wires were planted across the road and I was supposed to identify the wires. The instructors had just shown us the pictures of these wires sweeping across the path and the mine attached to them. I was pretty interested in learning how to identify those wires. If I missed one, an explosive charge would go off on the side of the trail to let me know that I had just blown it.

I tripped one of those wires and that thing went off. How do you suppose I finished the rest of the trail? On my hands and knees trying to find the next wire.

It had lots of realism to me because, as soon as those charges went off, the first thing that came to my mind was the picture I had seen of those men who had suffered in Vietnam.

The reason I share this with you is that we, in going to our church meetings, are taught to identify the pungie stick pits in our high schools, in our jobs, and in our business experiences. There are just as real *pungie stick pits* out there as there were in Vietnam. We can be taught to identify them just as surely as I was taught in my experience in basic training.

My good friend became what the army calls a Green Beret. He became a professional soldier. He went through jump school, became a paratrooper and ranger.

He was active in the Church. A strong, morally clean guy. A great young man. He found himself going to Vietnam. I was fortunate; when I got out of OCS, I was assigned to Europe because the particular missile I worked on wasn't in Vietnam; so I didn't have to go to Vietnam.

Because my friend stayed awake in those classes, he developed an ability to recognize those little wires and a pungie stick pit from twelve to fifteen feet away. Because he had this ability, when he'd take his squad out, he always brought them back alive. He carried in his pocket little popsicle sticks. He had a ribbon attached to each of them. He would go in front of the squad; and as he identified the wires and the mines, he would put a little stick next to it. As the rest of his squad would come by, they would see these little markings. They would heed the warning and would avoid the devastation of the mines and pungie sticks. He brought his guys back for eleven months without a failure. His men really developed a love and a respect for him because he helped save their lives. He would spot the danger before they would.

In the eleventh month that he was in Vietnam, he was coming down one of the trails and he took his eye off the trail for just a second. He missed one of those three-wire mines. His foot brushed one of those little wires and it went off. There wasn't enough left of him to send home.

The reason I share this experience with you is that his experience had great impact on me. My friend had listened, and he knew. Yet his error took his life.

We are in school for twelve years. We may last right up until the graduation party. But if we take our eyes off the goal that we are establishing in this training experience just for a moment, we're going to find ourselves lying in one of those pits experiencing just as real anguish, pain, and suffering as anybody did in Vietnam. We can equal that kind of pain when we make moral mistakes.

He Was a Nerd

There isn't anybody reading this book who doesn't know the difference between right and wrong—not anybody. We all know. But for some reason, when we get away from the warmth of an experience at church and we get away by ourselves, something happens. We begin to rationalize. We begin to want to be part of the group, don't we? Isn't there a pretty strong desire to be part of the in-group at school?

You young ladies will relate to this. There is usually a guy or several guys at your high school whom every girl would just absolutely slit their wrists to go out with.

One day this guy calls you up. He asks you to go to a dance with him. You're ecstatic. And when the other girls at the high school are coveting your date something fierce, you're going around saying, "Yes, nothing to it."

You go to the dance that night and you're in seventh heaven. You've been through all those training experiences and you know how to recognize all the pits.

At the dance he says, "Why don't we go to my house for a little while."

The little red flag goes up in your mind and you say, "Are your folks home?"

"Oh yeah, my folks are home. Don't worry. My folks are home."

And you think, "Well, maybe it will be all right."

So, you go over to his house. As you drive up and see the lights are all off in the house he says, "I guess my folks aren't home after all."

You are a little nervous about that, but you go into

the house. As you walk in, you notice the house is *all ready*. There are six records on the record player. There is something to drink on the tables, and the lights are turned down just right when you enter the room. What do you do? Well, if you adhere to the basic training that you've gone through, you see one big fat *pungie stick* in his living room, don't you?

And you look at him and say, "Look, Nerd, take me home. I don't go for this stuff at all."

Is it difficult to do that? You bet it is, because, when you go to school Monday morning, all the other girls run up and say, "Oh, how was it with *him*?"

And when you tell them that he was a nerd, they will say, "What do you mean, he's a nerd?"

"Well, he took me to his house and he wanted me to do things I don't believe in."

And they will say, "You're crazy."

Standing up to the crowd is not possible unless you've paid attention to the good basic training given at home and at church.

Lehi's Dream: Tree of Life

Is it difficult to be different from the crowd? Do you remember the story in the eighth chapter of First Nephi about the great and spacious building? Do you remember that story? What were the people in the building doing? What about the people who were at the tree, do you remember? The people in the building were pointing their fingers at *them*. They were scoffing and mocking.

There were saying things like, "You turkeys, what are you doing at that tree? This is where it's at, in the great and spacious building. I mean we've got rock bands and pot and all that good stuff. This is where it's at!"

And what did some of the people at the tree do? "They were ashamed." And they fell away and were lost into the building. That's what happens at our high schools, isn't it? The crowd comes up to us, puts their finger in our faces, and says, "You don't act like or think like we do. If you want to be happy here at this school, you'd better behave the way we do." Isn't that true?

If we're listening in these training experiences we can make it when the test comes. And there *is* going to be a test. If you wait until you're up the canyon and the windows are all fogged up, it's too late.

But if, on the way up the canyon, you say, "Hey, where are we going?"

"Well, I thought we'd go up to the canyon."

You say, "Hey, nerd, take me home."

That's what basic training does for you. You miss the pits. You don't end up with all the pain that goes with them. You all will have a chance to fail morally, and you will all have that opportunity often. I want to tell you young ladies, there are boys in your school that would have you if they could; young men there are girls in your school that would have you and enjoy bringing you down to their level.

The next time you have the opportunity and you're with one of those girls or young men, I want you to look at his or her forehead; and you know what you're going to see there? You're going to see a great big, green *pungie stick*. Look for the pungie stick and you will say, "Holy smoke, get me out of here."

Russian Army Tradition

The Russian army has a very interesting tradition. After the Russian soldier has gone through his training, a big party is held for him at the barracks. It is his coming-out party, and the tradition is that he has to demonstrate his manhood.

The Russian barracks are five to six stories high. They have great big windows, big enough for a man to stand in. The way a soldier can prove his manhood is by drinking all night. He gets absolutely stoned out of his mind. Becoming totally inebriated is part of the test because the soldier is to stand on the windowsill with his back to the five-story drop, and drink one more bottle of beer all the way down without falling out of the window. If he can, he has proved his manhood. Now isn't that slick? I don't know anything smarter in my whole life than that. The reason I tell you this is to introduce this phrase. I want you to memorize it:

> *He who leans out of a window to see how far he can lean without falling is a jackass.*

Will you remember that? When you decide that you can handle it, young people, that you can go up the canyon, you are leaning out the window just as surely as that Russian soldier was. Is that smart? Do smart people do that? No.

The second thing that you're going to see, the next time you have a chance to make a choice, is that drunken soldier leaning out the window.

Big Hunk Candy Bars

There was a bishop who was working with a young man who wanted to become part of the wrong group. He was not responding to the counsel of the bishop. He was not coming to his priesthood meetings anymore. And he had just purchased a brand new car. It was a '56 Chevrolet. Have you ever seen a '56 Chevrolet? There wasn't a finer car ever made.

With that new car, he felt as though he could do anything. The bishop invited this boy over to his house because he wasn't *getting to him*. The bishop spent three hours with this young man, pleading with him, talking about the pits and the direction the young man was going. The bishop just wasn't reaching him. He wasn't able to get to him at all.

Finally, the kid said, "I've got to go, Bishop." A little heartsick, the bishop walked the boy to his car.

As he walked from his house, the bishop saw the boy's beautiful '56 Chevrolet parked at the curb. He had an idea. The bishop said, "Will you wait just one more minute?"

"Sure."

The bishop went back into the house and found a *Big Hunk* candy bar. It's a big, long, white candy bar. Together they walked to the car. The bishop talked and at the same time, unwrapped the candy bar and unscrewed the gas cap of that beautiful car. The young man was watching all of this; but before he could do anything, the bishop dropped that candy bar into the gas tank.

He looked at the young man and said, "Good night." And walked into the house.

Finally, all that the bishop had been trying to tell him hit home. He realized, "That's what he's been trying to tell me. What I'm doing is the same thing this candy bar is going to do to my car." The car he worshipped he couldn't drive home. He had visions of the candy getting up into the carburetor and creating a mess.

He walked home. The bishop hadn't offered him a ride. What do you suppose he was thinking about all the time he walked? "I'll kill that Bishop."

He walked back the next day. He had to drain the gas. He had to take the gas tank down from the bottom of the car and take it apart and take out the candy bar. He had to put it back together and up underneath the car, and fill it with gas.

All the time he was doing that what do you suppose he was thinking? His whole life, that's what he was thinking about. He started to come back to Church because he didn't want his body, his life, to be like that car with the *Big Hunk* candy bar going through it.

Now, the third thing I want you to think about the next time you have a chance to fail—if you don't think of pungie sticks or Russian soldiers—is *Big Hunk* candy bars. There are three things now that you can recall. All of which, young people, can have great power and impact in helping you remember your basic training.

The Rape of Lucrece

This poem by William Shakespeare summarizes the way I feel about this challenge we have—to listen in our training sessions so that we can go out into the world and face dangerous pits and miss them. The story is about a man by the name of Lucius Tarquinius. He is thinking about raping the beautiful Lucrece. As he is contemplating this evil deed, the thoughts that go through his mind are what I want you to very carefully consider. I also want you to commit it to memory. Lucius said to himself:

> *What win I, if I gain the thing I seek.*
> *A dream, a breath, a froth of fleeting joy.*
> *Who buys a minute's mirth to wail a week?*
> *Or sells eternity to get a toy?*
> *For one sweet grape who will the vine destroy?*
> *Or what fond beggar, but to touch the crown,*
> *Would with the sceptre straight be strucken down?*
>
> William Shakespeare

Do you get the message of the poem, young people? Learn that, will you? Every time you have an opportunity to fail, think of the first line of that poem. *What win I, if I gain the thing I seek. A dream, breath, a froth of fleeting joy. Who buys a minute's mirth to wail a week?* What kind of people do that, young people? Dumb people, isn't that right? Dumb people. *Or, [who] sells eternity to get a toy?* What kind of people sell eternity to get a toy? Dumb people. Isn't that right? *For one sweet grape who will the vine destroy?* Now what kind of people would destroy the whole vine? Dumb people! This poem is about dumb people, my young friends.

Think about that as you have opportunity to fail, will you? What win I if I do this thing?—a dream, a breath, a froth of fleeting momentary pleasure? Who buys a minute's mirth to wail a week? Dumb people. Or, for one sweet grape, who will the vine destroy? Not you, I hope.

Follow the counsel of Shakespeare. Follow the counsel of your advisors, your parents, your bishop, your stake president. Avoid the pits. As a bishop, I had the task and responsibility on a number of occasions of having to pull some of my young people out of those pits. It is no fun. It is ugly. I had to witness the pain and the anguish they went through. I'd give anything to prevent you from having to go through the same pain.

The Lord paid for our sins. He experienced the pain and the anguish for us. If we will just allow Him in our lives, allow Him to pay for our mistakes, we don't have to go through the pain. If we choose to go through the pain anyway, what kind of people are we? Dumb people. You are smart. You are wiser than that.

Will you learn that, young people? I plead with you to stay close to the Lord. Avoid the pits. Experience all of the blessings that come from obeying the principles of the gospel. Obey whether you want to or not. If you obey for obedience's sake—if that's why you're obeying—you will still get the blessings; and as you mature and grow and look back, you'll be able to say, "Thank God I obeyed, because now I understand why the Lord asked me to keep myself clean."

I bear witness of the gospel of Jesus Christ, for it is true. The Lord lives. He loves you. He knows who you are. He has a job for you to perform, but He needs you clean. Remember the pits. Remember the Russian soldiers leaning out of windows. Remember candy bars. Remember the poem from Shakespeare and you will stay clean. Some day you will look back and be very happy that you did.

I have more confidence in asking for the Lord's help because I am doing all I can to obey His commandments.

THE REVEREND

As our faith increases so does our ability to obey.

Three personal experiences have provided great learning opportunities for me. The basic principle I learned was that faith is more than doing. It is a gift from God which is increased through our obedience to true principles; and as we obey, we are blessed with more faith.

The Fort Polk Reverend

When I returned from my mission in 1965 from London, England, I received one of those letters which reads like this: "Congratulations, your friends and neighbors have selected you to represent them in the United States Army." I have been looking for those people ever since.

I went to a place called Fort Polk, Louisiana. I don't know if you have ever heard of Fort Polk; but when the world ends, it is going to start at Fort Polk. It's a bad place. I received my basic training at Fort Polk. During basic training, the military takes a bright, vibrant young American mind and, in eight weeks reduces it to an undulating blob of green protoplasm.

When I arrived, they took all my hair away, gave me a green suit and a rifle, and said they were going to teach me to be a killer. Here I was, just off my mission, and now I was going to be a killer. Because the Vietnam War was rising at such a great pace there were lots of people going through basic training. The barracks were overcrowded. I don't know if you've ever seen a military barrack before, but it is very basic living.

It has a roof, four walls, and two stories. Forty young men are normally put on each floor; but because of the war, we had sixty. There were double-deck bunks down both sides of the barracks. The double-deck bunks were about two to three feet apart. When I went to bed, I had to sorta slip in sideways and shimmy into bed. There was a wide center corridor with footlockers lined up and down both sides.

I was assigned to the top bunk at the far right-hand corner of the room. At ten-thirty that first night I was feeling a little humiliated—no hair and this green suit and everything. As I was about to climb into bed, it dawned on me that it was time for Elder Smith to say his prayers. I looked around and there wasn't anybody else praying. I stood there for probably twelve minutes wrestling with myself with all the reasons why it would be okay for me to leap into bed and say one on my back.

I said to myself, "Surely the Lord wouldn't mind. After all, it's really difficult to kneel from the top bunk. I think He would understand that."

I was going through this rationalization process and, finally after about twelve minutes, Elder Smith said to me, "You've just come from England, Elder Smith, where you have been telling people for two years that it was critical to get on their knees and talk to the Lord every night." I decided that I had better do it.

The fellow who slept underneath me had already gone to bed. I bent down and tapped him on the shoulder. "Would you mind if I used your bunk to say my prayers?"

He looked at me as if I was from another planet and answered, "Okay." He got up and left.

I never understood why he had to leave but he didn't want to be there while I was praying. I knelt down and said my prayers. I don't actually remember if I prayed or not, but I do remember kneeling down. I can remember a very uneasy silence for about a two-bed radius. I could feel the fingers pointing at me and imagined such comments as, "What's he doing?"

It got a little easier the next night. The morning after that first night, I was named the *Reverend*. In fact I was called Reverend for the rest of my military experience.

The next night it was easier to pray on my knees. I developed a little ritual with the fellow under me. I would tap him on the shoulder and he would get up and leave. On the fourth night, one of the fellows came up while I was praying and said, "Hey, can I help you find what you're looking for?"

I said, "No thanks. I'm saying my prayers." You should have seen the look on his face.

The soldier who slept in the bed next to mine was a fellow by the name of Osmond. Osmond was from Kentucky. He stood six-foot-five and weighed two hundred and forty pounds; there was no fat on Osmond. He had mastered the military vocabulary which means he had a foul mouth. Because of his size, he got what he wanted.

On the fifth day he approached me out on one of the training ranges and said, "Reverend, I want to talk to you."

I said, "Lay it on me."

"I've been thinking; I'd really like you to pray for me. I've been watching you pray each night. Would you mind praying for me?"

I figured if anybody needed praying for, Osmond did. So I answered, "Sure, Osmond, I'd be glad to pray for you."

That night as I was about to pray, he said, "Don't forget, Reverend, you're going to pray for me tonight."

"Sure, Osmond." So I did. I prayed for Osmond.

The next day, we were out on the range again. He came up to me and said, "Reverend, something else has been bothering me and I need to talk to you."

I looked at him and said, "All right."

We walked off where we could be alone. He said, "Reverend, isn't it a little noisy in the barracks when you pray at night?"

Beginning to get a little nervous I looked up at him and said, "Yes. I have to admit I've prayed in quieter places. Why?"

"Well, I want you to tell me when you're ready to pray tonight."

I looked at him with a question on my face and said, "Okay, Osmond. Whatever you say."

I must not have wanted to tell Osmond when I was going to pray, because I forgot. At ten thirty that night when I was getting ready for bed, he walked over and said, "Reverend, you ready to pray?"

"It's time, Osmond."

He proceeded to walk out into the center corridor of the barrack and yelled out seven of the foulest words you can imagine and then said, "I want it quiet in here."

In less than a second, you could hear a pin drop. All sixty of the young men on my floor came out to the edge of their bunks and looked down the aisle to where Osmond stood. Next to his six-foot-five frame stood the Reverend.

Osmond continued, "I want it quiet in here while the Reverend prays." He looked over at me and said, "Pray."

There wasn't anything else for the Reverend to do, so I knelt down to pray in perfect silence for the first time since I had been there.

That turned out to be a marvelous experience. For the next eight weeks, I could not have gone to bed without praying if I had wanted to, but I had to meet Osmond's schedule. One night I was in the shower and had to come out and pray wet because it was time to meet Osmond's schedule. The whole thing was a fun time. At prayer time, Osmond would get it quiet, I'd come up to pray; they would call me Reverend and I would call them the Brethren. It was a great experience.

The thing that turned the exercise into one of the most sobering ones of my life occurred the last day of training. It is a day for a parade and awards. I was given a marksman's badge for hitting a target with four thousand rounds from a machine gun.

After the parade, I discovered that seventeen of the young men on my floor were members of the Church. All seventeen of them were from the state of Utah. All of them had been active in the Church up until the day they had come into the army. Most of them had lost their virtue in Leesville, a nasty little pit outside of Fort Polk. Most of them were smoking and/or drinking. Most of them had mastered the military vocabulary. Do you know how I found out? Each of them felt it necessary before they left to come and apologize. Seventeen times that afternoon these young men, handsome, strong-looking, would come by and say to me: "Reverend, I think there's something you ought to know. I'm LDS too, and I'm not very proud of it today."

I had to ride from Fort Polk to Jackson, Mississippi, to get an airplane. I'll never forget that bus ride as long as I live. I wept as I pled with the Lord. "Why, why, Lord? What happens to a young man who goes through the programs of the Church? He goes through Seminary, Sunday School, Primary, and all the marvelous things that are available to him; and when he comes into the military, he blows it."

Do you know what the answer is? There arrives a time in all our lives when we have to find out for ourselves if the Church is true. We can't bask in our father's light any more or our mother's or our bishop's or our stake president's. We've got to know for ourselves.

The message in the military, when you get there, is, "If you want to be happy here, my friend, you've got to do what we do. You've got to think like we think. You've got to act like we act. You've got to do all the things we do. And if you don't want to do these things, you'd better not plan on being very happy here. You're not going to be *in*. And if you're not in, it's no fun."

That is incredible pressure and many succumb to it. They don't make it. That is why I have a compelling sense of urgency for each of us.

Young people, I beg and plead with you to find your own testimonies—to find out for yourselves if God lives, to find out that the Book of Mormon really is the word of God—because somebody one day is going to stand you up against the wall and ask you, "Do you really believe that?"

Arty: My Friend in New York

I had an experience like that while I lived in New York City some years ago. At that time I was a young man who aspired to be a missionary. I was living with a very dear friend of mine who was not a member of the Church. We came home one night after working late. He proceeded to tell me about his faith. He was a brilliant young man who has since graduated from Cornell University in oceanography. He has a doctor's degree in that discipline. He is a bright, bright guy.

He told me about his church and finished with this comment, "You know, religion is great for kids and old people, but we don't need it, do we? We're so slick, we just don't need it. Now tell me about the Mormon Church."

I began by telling him the Joseph Smith story. I had a very interesting experience when I told my very close, dear friend, Arty Gaines, that great story. It made me nervous.

I said, "Well, you know, there was this kid in upstate New York. . ." I started to sweat, because when I said, "upstate New York," I realized I was in New York City and only a couple hundred miles from Palmyra.

"You know," I continued, "he wanted to join a church, so he went out to a forest by his dad's farm and knelt down to pray. While he was praying, this great light came down."

Arty's eyes got as big as frisbees.

I struggled on, "This light came down and shone all around, and he looked up and there were two men standing in the light."

Arty, very quickly said, "Yeah, who was it?"

I said with some difficulty, "Well, actually, it was God and Christ."

"You mean they've been to New York?"

That was a jolt.

I said, "I guess they have." I had never thought about it quite like that before.

I proceeded to get off the subject as quickly as I could and finished my story. Arty was completely blown away by the story. I'll never forget what he said as long as I live.

His eyes never got any smaller after I'd finished this wild tale. He looked at me and said, "Hyrum, do you really believe that?"

The response that I had been conditioned all my life to give almost popped out, "Of course I believe that." (How dare you even ask me if I believed that.)

Because of the close relationship we had—we were like brothers—I had to look him in the eye and say, "You know, Arty, nobody ever asked me that before. You know, I don't know for sure if it's true."

Then his eyes returned to their normal size and he said, "Boy, I'm sure glad. You had me worried for a moment. That's the wildest story I've ever heard." He then rolled over and went to sleep.

Now, my eyes were as big as frisbees. I lay there that night a very shaken young man. I said to myself, "Suppose it's not true. (Whew, heavy!) Maybe I had better find out. My family has been a part of this for a long time. Maybe I don't know for myself if it's true."

I woke up the next morning with a powerful desire to find out. I began reading, thinking, experimenting, and praying like I had never done before in my life. I won't tell you how long it took; but over a period of years I developed a testimony that was *mine*. I gained enough of one to go on a mission and there it solidified and became much stronger.

Several years later I went back to New York, took a special trip, and invited Arty Gaines to dinner. As we were eating, I said, "Remember that story I told you about the light and the two men?"

"Yes, I remember the story."

"It's true. I want you to know, Arty, that I know that it is true just as surely as I sit here tonight." His eyes didn't get big this time. He knew that I knew. I went on, "You've got to admit either that it's true or it's not. Would you buy that?"

"Yeah, I'd buy that."

"As a son of God, you owe it to yourself to find out."

So far Arty hasn't done anything with that challenge, but he knows that I know for sure that it is true. I would like everyone reading this book to find out for themselves. If you'll do that, then it won't make any difference what happens to anyone else's testimony including the prophet's. Nothing can shake the testimony that the Lord has given you as a gift. Testimonies are gifts from our Father in Heaven, but we must earn the gift.

In acquiring your testimony, great spiritual strength will come to you. Your faith will increase and great power will be yours, more power to cope with this world than you ever dreamed.

OCS: Proud to be a Mormon

The army for me was a great experience. I decided to get married while in the army. My wife's father did not want her to marry a private so I went to Officer's Candidate School and earned a commission in the army Artillery. At OCS the army takes an enlisted man and, in twenty-three weeks, turns him into an officer. It is very rigorous and demanding training. During the last three weeks, our rank at OCS was determined by class standing. I was fortunate to be honor graduate of my class. I was the top-ranking candidate.

I had four diamonds on my shoulder. That meant I was a candidate general. I had more power in OCS than I ever had in the real army. I was demoted to a second lieutenant when I graduated.

My title was regimental commander. There were seven men on the regimental staff. They were the top seven candidates in the entire school. There were all different ranks—three diamonds, two diamonds, one diamond—in fact, diamonds all over the place.

One night we were sitting in our staff office. A brand new class of candidates had just come into the school. We were reviewing the personal data contained on the new candidates' three-by-five cards. One of my staff members raised a card and laughingly said, "We've got another one."

"We got another what?" I said.

"We've got another reverend."

The staff thought that was great, and they laughed about it and joked as he handed me the card. I looked at the card, and sure enough in the bottom right-hand corner I read, "Religious preference: LDS, language spoken: French." That told me something.

One of the fellows looked at me and, in a sort of half-serious way, said, "Reverend, do you suppose this new candidate is as proud of being a Mormon as you are?"

"Of course he is," I said. "If he's a Mormon, he's proud of it."

They joked and kidded me for several minutes. Then one of them said in a serious tone, "Reverend, how would you like to prove that to us."

I said, "Sure. Follow me."

To fully appreciate the challenge, you have to know something about OCS. There isn't anything more fearful than upperclassmen. The lowerclassmen hated, despised, and feared upperclassmen, especially the regimental staff. We wore horseshoe taps on our shoes. Have you seen these horseshoe taps? You could hear an upperclassman coming for blocks. We had our own passes. We walked wherever we wanted. The lowerclassmen had to jump across our walk, for if they ever got caught walking on an upper class sidewalk, it was death.

We put on our uniforms, our cleats, shined up our brass, and then marched to the barracks where this new class was getting ready for bed. It was about ten in the evening. We walked in the barracks and, as is the military tradition, the first candidate that saw our diamonds screamed at the top of his lungs, "Attention!"

Everybody in the barracks froze into a rigid position of attention.

Another thing you have to understand about OCS is that the barracks are a little different than the real Army. The floors are so highly shined we could see our faces in them. They get that way because lowerclassmen shined them with wax and water on their hands and knees. The lowerclassmen were not allowed to walk on their own floor. If they wanted to get to their bed, they would have to crawl across the tops of their beds with their shoes under their arms. The only people allowed to walk on the floors are the upperclassmen.

We walked into the barracks, down the center aisle with our cleats, and just destroyed the shine on the floor. Of course, we intended to do that because we knew it would take them all night to get the floor repolished for inspection in the morning. We walked up and down the aisle for a few minutes, thoroughly intimidating these brand new OCS candidates. They thought they were in for real trouble because here, on their first day, was the entire regimental staff.

I stopped and stood at one end of the barracks. I mustered one of my gruffer voices and said, "I want to know if there are any Mormons in here." You could have heard a pin drop. I could see each candidate sneak a look, wondering if anyone dared admit it.

Down at one end of the hall, a hand went up. I took a deep breath, and all seven of us stomped there with our noisy cleated shoes. I walked into the cubicle of Chuck Bailey. I had never seen him before in my life. He had never seen me either. I walked up to Chuck and put my nose three inches from his nose and said, "I want to know if you're a Mormon?"

"Yes, sir." He said without a moment of hesitation.

"Are you proud to be a Mormon?"

"Yes, sir!"

Then I said, "I'm sure glad; I'm Hyrum Smith." He fell apart. He put his arms around me and I put my arms around him. We just hugged each other for a moment. I kept my arm around him and turned to my staff and said, in not a very humble way, "I told you so."

They shrugged and said, "Oh brother, we've got another reverend."

Then I introduced myself to the rest of the candidates that were still standing at attention in the room. I said, "I want you to watch Chuck Bailey. Six months from now he's going to graduate wearing four diamonds."

I turned to Chuck and said, "Thanks, Chuck." I shook his hand and I left. I have never seen him since.

However, six months later I couldn't stand the suspense. I was in Germany. I wrote Colonel Howard, the commandant of OCS, and discovered, sure enough, Chuck Bailey had graduated with four diamonds.

I'll never forget as long as I live the majesty of that young man standing there, never having seen me before, not knowing what was coming. That was a tremendously pressured experience. Unequivocally saying, "Yes sir, I'm a Mormon and I don't care who you are or who knows it. I am a Mormon and I'm proud of it."

Where does that kind of strength come from? It comes from having your own testimony; and as that testimony grows, faith grows, courage comes with the faith, and miracles happen.

The Man, the Wind, and the Cliff

There was a man standing on a very high cliff, about nine hundred feet from the ground. He was looking over the great expanse when a great wind came up and blew him off the cliff.

As he fell, he anticipated the greasy spot he would

make at the bottom. He cried out, "Oh Lord, don't let me die."

Suddenly a branch appeared upon the side of the cliff, and he reached out and grabbed it. There he hung five hundred feet from the bottom and four hundred feet from the top. He couldn't climb up and he couldn't climb down. He was wondering what he was going to do.

As he hung there, a voice whispered in his ear very softly, "Believest thou that I created the wind that blew you off this cliff?"

Very quickly the man replied, "Yea, Lord, thou knowest I believe."

There was a long pause before the voice whispered a second time, "Believest thou that I created the branch that broke your fall and saved your life?"

Very quickly the man said, "Yea, Lord, thou knowest I believe."

Then the pause seemed even longer and the voice whispered a third time, this time almost imperceptibly, "Believest thou that I could create a wind that would blow you back up to the top of the cliff?"

"Yea, Lord, thou knowest I believe."

Then several hours went by before the voice whispered a fourth time, this time so low he could barely hear it. The voice said, "Let go."

We are in that position. The Lord is asking us to let go. Do you have the faith to let go? You know what Paul would have done? He would have opened his hand and enjoyed the ride back up to the top.

I hear people saying all the time, "Yea, Lord, thou knowest I believe, but don't ask me to walk across the street and tell my neighbors that I love them. Yea, Lord, thou knowest I believe, but don't ask me to do my visiting teaching. No, that's too much."

My testimony is that the miracle is not going to

occur until we, the members of the Church, acquire testimonies that are our own. As we do this, the faith will come, and as faith comes, the miracle will happen. But miracles won't happen until we build the rocks; and the rocks are our desire, our ability, our tenacity in going out and doing what the Lord has asked us to do.

I want you to know that I know the gospel of Jesus Christ is true. I know that Joseph Smith did see, and did stand with, God and Jesus Christ. They have given us the most powerful, magnificent message in the world today. I plead with you to make this message known to the world—to strengthen yourselves inside so that, when the heat comes and the opportunities surface (and they usually come simultaneously), you'll be able to stand to do what the Lord has sent you and prepared you and given you the talents to do.

I am proud to tell people I am a Mormon because my faith increases as I personally practice each principle of the gospel.

WALK ACROSS THE STREET

Sharing with others what we have only increases what we have and know.

My family and I had an experience that taught us a great lesson about being missionaries.

The Four-hundred-mile-wide Street

When we lived in Portland, I had the opportunity of being in a stake presidency. I was asked by the stake president, on one occasion, to speak about missionary work at the Saturday evening session of stake conference. I gave what I thought was a terrific talk on why members ought to do missionary work.

It was obvious during the talk that I wasn't getting the message through to the stake. All I did was increase the guilt trip most of us are on when it comes to really doing anything about missionary work.

My wife and I came home that night, and I was very frustrated. I was stomping around the house saying, "Sweetheart, why can't we get the people of this stake to just walk across the street to their neighbors and ask them to come into their home for a home evening and tell them they love them? Why won't they do that? What's so tough about that?"

I was stomping around exhibiting all kinds of righteous indignation. Gail just sat there with an interesting kind of a smile on her face. I made the mistake of asking one more question. "Sweetheart, why do you suppose we haven't done it yet?"

That was my mistake. I will never forget her response. She pointed her finger at my nose, as only a wife can do, and said, "Would you really like me to tell you why we haven't done it yet, President?"

I said, "Yes. Tell me why."

"Because you are afraid to."

I was offended by that and offered my excuses, "Me? Your dragon slayer, President Smith? I'm not afraid of anything! I think you forgot I was on a mission for two years in England. I knocked on thousands of doors. I'm not afraid."

"You're afraid, President."

"Now wait a minute, Sweetheart. I know how to knock on doors."

"I dare you to go across the street right now and invite the McDowels over for a home evening."

I wasn't about to go across the street. And you know why? I was scared. I was afraid to. For the first time in my life, I recognized the emotion that kept me from going across my street. As I remembered that, I asked myself the question, "Why wasn't I afraid in England? Why wasn't I afraid when I knocked on the doors in England?"

You know why? I didn't live on any of those streets in England. If I had a bad experience on one of those streets, I would never have to go back. I would go to another street. You bet! But on my street, if I go across and embarrass myself with my neighbor, what happens? I would have to go to work early and come home late at night so he wouldn't see me anymore. It makes a difference when we live on the street, doesn't it?

At that point I learned something about myself. I remembered the way I got over that fear in the mission field. I had to go before the Lord and get a little extra help. I also learned something about the fact that you can't be afraid in front of your family. Dad's not afraid, is he?

So I got up in front of my family the next Monday night and said, "I've been thinking that we really ought to go across the street and maybe take some cookies to our neighbors and sing a song and tell them we love them and see if they would like to come to a home evening."

You know children aren't afraid. They got all excited about the idea. "Oh Dad, that's great! Let's do it tonight. Let's do it tonight, Dad."

"Well, I thought we'd do it next Monday night."

"Oh no, Dad. Let's do it tonight."

I looked at my wife and her finger started to come up.

"Okay, we'll do it tonight."

We prepared some cookies. We learned a song to sing and then we came into the front room for a word of prayer together. We then began the arduous journey across the street.

Do you have any idea how wide the streets are in Portland? It seemed like it took us about forty-five minutes to cross it. We walked up to the door of our neighbor directly across the street. My children pushing me out in front, we rang the doorbell. I deserved an *Oscar* for my performance that night.

The door opened and Mr. McDowel said, "Yes?"

I said, "Mr. McDowel, I'm Hyrum Smith and this is my wife and my children. We want you to know we love you. We prepared a song and made some cookies, and we'd like to come in and give you these cookies and sing you a song. May we do that?" What do you suppose his reaction was?

He had to go ask his wife for permission. He said, "Just a moment." He went back into the house and we could hear him whispering through the door.

He said, "Sweetheart, the people from across the street are out here. He said he loved me. They've got some cookies and they want to come in and sing a song."

"Sure, that's all right."

So he came back to the door and said, "Come on in."?!

And in walked the *lepers*. We felt like lepers because that is how they looked at us as we walked into the house that night.

We sang our song and presented our cookies. We had a marvelous experience. We invited them to come to a home evening; and to my horror, they said, "Yes." They went on, "Sure. We would love to do that."

I think they were emotionally curious, I mean really curious.

We left after we told them that we loved them again and walked back across the street. It didn't take us near as long to get back as it did to get over there.

What do you suppose Dad did when we got back into the safety and warmth of our living room? I stood before my family and said, "There wasn't anything to that, was there?"

"Oh Dad, that was great!" They wanted to go to another neighbor right then. I couldn't handle two in the same evening.

We started to have some marvelous experiences on our street with our neighbors. We saw some of them join the Church and saw them start to participate in the marvelous blessings that we have in the Church. I think we all recognize that there is just a little bit of fear in doing missionary work. In my case, there is a whole lot of fear. We can ask the Lord for help and we will overcome our fear.

When we went to Ventura as mission president, we found that the street in Ventura was just as wide as the street in Portland. We had to cross it the same way: prayer, cookies, the whole business, including Dad up front. And when we went across the street, we had great experiences in Ventura. We had a number of people going to church and going to home evenings. It was a great, great experience.

Our kids weren't afraid. There were thirty-seven kids who lived on our street in Ventura, and they all lived at our house. I don't know if it was good or bad. I think we carried it a little far, but they were all at our house. I would come home anytime to all thirty-seven kids running around. It was like a jungle. That is the exciting thing about doing missionary work, if it's going to happen and happen well, we have got to be in condition for it.

The greatest statement I've ever heard on missionary work or on fellowshipping is this:

Alone in the moonlight is better when you're not.

If you are standing on a cliff overlooking a beautiful moonlit scene, you can enjoy it to a degree. But if your wife is with you, wow! And if your family is with you, double wow! And if your whole street is there, triple wow! That is the essence of getting excited about sharing the gospel.

Do you have any idea of the impact on the world if the members of the Church became as excited about sharing their testimonies of the truth as they were about the recent hit movie? Incredible! That is what the prophet is asking of us—to get enthusiastic about the gospel.

There is a conditioning process that gets us from where we are going now to the point where we can, with some courage, walk across the four-hundred-mile-wide street and tell our neighbors that we love them. If you want an interesting experience, go to the man that you work next to—next office or whatever—walk in and shake his hand and say, "Sam, I love you." See what he does. He may look at you a little funny at first; but after about ten days of it, he will get hooked on it. You forget one day and he will come into your office and say, "How come you didn't tell me you loved me today?" He's going through withdrawal.

You ladies know what that's like. If your husband doesn't tell you he loves you four or five times a day, you go through withdrawal. I can tell by the way the phone rings that it is my wife and I've missed. I just pick up the phone and say, "I love you." She says, "Thanks," and I hang the phone back up.

I bought her a watch for Christmas one year, one of these digital watches, you know, where you push it once and it gives you the time, you push it twice and it gives you the date, you push it three times and it punches out "I love you." Great little watch. It saved me a big phone bill.

We all go through withdrawal, don't we, if we don't get love? When we start to achieve love, attention, consideration in our lives, we bask in it. That is what the whole fellowshipping process is about.

How do we get into condition for it? I suggest to you that if we are going to be decent emissaries of our Father in Heaven, we have got to be the best at what we do. I don't think there is any greater compliment that can be paid to anyone than for a peer to tell someone that he or she is really good. Do you believe that? You've heard actors and actresses say, "Boy, he is good." Or, "Have you seen him? He really is good."

I believe if we are the best at what we do, it says a whole lot to a lot of people. If we are going to be the best at what we do, we've also got to be best in our responsibility as sons and daughters of God in acquiring testimonies of the gospel. How do we get from where we are to where we want to be? We have to put forth energy. Everything worthwhile takes effort.

Sharing Starts with a Testimony

We have to have our own testimony. It takes effort on our part—prayer, learning, study, thinking, experimenting with the gospel. This is the way our testimony starts. With testimony comes a thing called faith. As faith becomes a part of our lives the miracles begin. But how do we get more faith? Faith is courage. Faith is the ability to walk across the street, walk into the next office, take every opportunity to bear our testimonies.

Why is it important to gain our own testimony? I want you to know that in every age of time since the beginning of this earth, when the Church of Christ has been perceived by the sons of men as a political and economical power, the persecution has started and risen in direct proportion to that perceived economical and political threat.

When Christ was on the earth, the Sanhedrin and the Romans were a lot more concerned about the numbers of people that were beginning to follow him than what he taught. They couldn't deal with his popularity, so they got rid of him.

When Joseph Smith and the Saints were beginning to grow, the opposition didn't like what he taught. But even more, they didn't like that he was a serous candidate for the presidency of the United States. In Illinois, they believed he could be elected. Governor Thomas Ford was afraid of the Mormons. Nauvoo was the most beautiful city in Illinois, much larger than Chicago. The persecution increased as the strength of the Church increased.

I suggest to you that the Church is becoming a political and economical threat today. The persecution is beginning again. Subtly perhaps, but it is beginning again.

Brigham Young stood in front of the people in Nauvoo and said, "I want you to follow me. We are going to this really neat place out West. I'm not really sure where we are going, but it's out there and it's neat and I want you to go with me."

How many people do you suppose went with Brigham Young? A good percentage of the membership did not follow Brigham Young. Do you know why? Have you ever asked yourself why? Because it wasn't comfortable to follow Brigham Young. Those who didn't go would say, "Leave my beautiful home here in Nauvoo? Go out there in a wagon? No way!"

How many people do you suppose pay a full tithing in the Church today? About 30 percent. How many go to sacrament meeting on a regular basis? About 33 percent. How many hold regular family home evenings? About 35 percent. Why? Because we have not acquired the ability to find out for ourselves that the gospel of Jesus Christ is true. We can't bask in somebody else's light. We can be strengthened by it; but when we are sitting on the hearth all by ourselves, we have to have light of our own or our light will go out. There are a whole lot of lights going out because people can't reach your light or someone else's light.

A Coal from the Fire

I had an experience some years ago when I was a bishop. A young man came up to me and said, "Bishop, I want you to tell me why we go to all the meetings we do. I've got to go to Seminary, Sunday School, and all of these meetings. I'm tired of it. You tell me why we go to these meetings."

As that young man asked that question, I thought back to an experience I had as a youth when I went to a fireside. It was a real, live fireside because there was a fire really burning.

The man who was speaking that night got up and said, "I'm going to talk tonight about why we go to all the meetings we go to."

He proceeded to walk across the room to the fire. He reached into the fire with a two-pronged poker and pulled a coal out of the fire—a great big, beautiful, red glowing coal. He put it down on the hearth, walked back to his seat, and sat down. He crossed his legs, folded his arms, and watched the coal. There wasn't anything else for us to do, so we sat and watched the coal, too.

We watched it for about twenty minutes. That coal, as you would imagine, started to get dimmer and dimmer; and pretty soon it started to smoke. You know how coal gets black as it cools. So it was cold. Then he got up and walked across the room and picked the coal up with his bare hand. I was impressed with that. He set this coal back into the fire. Then he walked back and sat down. He didn't say a word. He just watched the coal. As you would imagine, the coal started to get a little brighter and a little brighter and pretty soon it was just as red and beautiful as all the other coals.

He then got up and said, "That's my talk, amen."

That was the greatest talk I have ever witnessed. That talk had more impact upon me, I think, than any talk I had ever heard up to that night. That is why we attend all the meetings we do. We don't go to sacrament meeting on Sunday just to attend another meeting. We go to that sacrament meeting so that we can bask in each other's light. These meetings are stoking experiences to stir us up, to fire us with the Spirit. We come—not because there is going to be a great speaker or a bad speaker—we come because we can be together. We can sit by each other, and we can share in each other's strengths and our *coal* is stoked. We can go away from the fire for the rest of the week, and we can feel its strength.

I answered that young man's question with a question. "What did you have for dinner three weeks ago on Thursday night?"

He said, "Bishop, I can't remember what I had for dinner today. That's a dumb question."

"Did it do you any good?"

"Of course it did me some good. It kept me alive another day."

"That's right. That is why we go to all these meetings. Because they keep us alive another day spiritually."

I would hope that we not only go to meetings to be stirred by the speakers; but, just sitting together, we feel each other's light. That is what people feel when they come to church for the first time.

You will not long remember what you read or what you may hear in church meetings, but you will never forget what you feel.

That is the power of the fellowshipping program. People will come into your home for a family home evening, and they will feel something there. They don't know what it is yet—the Spirit of God—but they will go away from that experience and they will want more of it.

That same principle applies not only to sharing the gospel with nonmembers; but also, as we learn to share our time and our talents, we discover a marvelous miracle. When we share ourselves, we expand our horizons and our abilities are increased. Our real success comes because we care enough for ourselves and others to share whatever we have with them.

I am learning so much from others because I am sharing what I know with them.

LAUNDRY LISTS

Following the Lord's laundry lists helps us keep our own laundry clean.

There are some great words which the scriptures lead us to that define change. I won't list all of them, but let me give you two lists of scriptures and six words—laundry lists, I like to call them—of characteristics that describe the Ammon type. The people who have already created the change and have become like Christ are people who can answer the questions we discussed in the first chapter in the affirmative.

"Yes, I have spiritually been born of God. Yes, I have received His image in my countenance. Yes, I have experienced the mighty change in my heart; and yes, I can still feel it. Why can I? Because I'm doing all the things that would allow me to still feel it."

I'm going to give you my negative list first, and then I'm going to give you my positive list. I want you to study these two lists. The negative list is shorter than the positive one. The first lists things which the Lord does not like. In the sixth chapter of Proverbs, the Lord gives us seven things that he hates.

Laundry List Number One: Negative

In verse sixteen of chapter six in Proverbs, we read, "These six things doth the Lord hate: Yea, seven are an abomination unto Him."

1. "A proud look." The Lord doesn't like that. What is a proud look? Have you ever seen a proud look? Have you ever been so excited to see somebody and when you have approached them to shake hands, they didn't have time for you? Then, there is that inactive member who has been smoking for thirty years and finally gets up the nerve to come to church and somebody walks up and says, "What are you doing here?" He is crushed and never comes back. A proud look.

2. "A lying tongue." We know what that is.

3. "Hands that shed innocent blood." We know what that is, too.

4. "An heart that deviseth wicked imaginations." What is a heart that deviseth wicked imaginations? You know what wicked imaginations are.

5. "Feet that be swift in running to mischief." One night while in the mission field, we had gone to bed when we heard a noise outside. We got up and parted the curtains. Six missionaries were toilet-papering the mission home. "Feet that be swift in running to mischief." The Lord doesn't like that.

6. "A false witness that speaketh lies."

7. "He that soweth discord among brethren." Have you ever known anyone that soweth discord among brethren? The Lord doesn't like any of those things.

These seven items are the negative side. Make a list and put it some place where you see it often—the refrigerator perhaps. Look at them periodically and say, "Do I do any of those?"

Now, let's consider what I like to call the *good list*.

There are lots of both kinds of lists in the scriptures. In the first book of Corinthians, chapter thirteen, Paul beautifully describes the principle of charity. Do you remember charity? *Charity is the pure love of Christ.*

What does that mean? What is the pure love of Christ? Let's bring it down for us lay folk to understand. Selflessness, patience. Let me give what I think is a great definition:

Charity:	The ability to love the sinner and hate the sin.

Can you do that? If you are driving down a freeway and you're late for class and some clown cuts in front of you, almost causing you to have an accident. If you had a little button on your steering wheel that would produce a laser beam that would destroy that automobile, would you use it?

Charity is the ability to love the sinner—the guy who cuts in front of you—and hate the sin—the act of driving in front of you. If you have mastered that, you can wave out of the window with all your fingers and say, "Hi." That is what charity is, okay?

Laundry List Number Two: The Good List

Paul gives us fifteen positive characteristics for charity in verses four through eight.

Charity:
1. Suffereth long.
2. Is kind.
3. Envieth not.
4. Vaunteth not itself.
5. Is not puffed up.
6. Doth not behave itself unseemly (improperly, indecently)
7. Seeketh not her own.
8. Is not easily provoked. (What does that mean? That means we don't reach for the laser beam.)

Remember, we are going to put this list on our refrigerator and we're going to look at it. For those who are married, if you want to have a great experience sometime, ask your sweetheart how you are doing on the list.

"Well, you're doing great, but go back to number eight and reread it." Great experience.

9. Charity thinketh no evil. That is the antithesis of an heart that deviseth wicked imaginations. Thinketh no evil.

Measure your performance. Remember, we are going to improve our self-thinking and self-talking (see the chapter on *Eye of Faith*). If you want to have charity, you'd better first see yourself as one having charity, like the Savior. A lot of people say, "Be like the Savior? You're kidding! Nobody can be like the Savior." And they stay in the mud all their lives.

10. Rejoiceth not in iniquity.
11. Rejoiceth in the truth.
12. Beareth all things.
13. Believeth all things.
14. Hopeth all things.
15. Endureth all things. (Endureth all things—even math.)

That's what charity is. A great list for character development.

There are six words which, if you reflect upon their meaning, will add to your self-perception. Internalize these definitions, and you're going to develop a courage you never had before. That courage is going to make you do things you've never done before. That will be very exciting to you.

Laundry List Number Three: Word Definitions.

The first word is wisdom.

Wisdom: *Knowledge rightly applied.*

We make a big issue out of that. We assimilate knowledge every day. We go to church classes; we go to college classes. We assimilate lots of knowledge. Whether or not we do anything with that knowledge is a measure of our wisdom. One of the emotions you are really going to have to wrestle with after reading this book is, "Am I going to do anything with what I've learned?" There is going to be a real fear to do it. A real fear.

The next word is charity. We've already discussed it at some length. However, I will include it again here so that you will associate the six word definitions together.

Charity: The ability to love the sinner and hate the sin.

If you internalize and understand the power of that statement, what that will do for your personal power will scare you. That means you have the maturity to separate behavior from the human being. If you really have charity, no one can ever get to you again. No one can ever put you down, because you are drawing on a source of power they don't even understand. You have learned to separate what they have done or said from them, the human being. You don't have to like what they have done, but you do continue to love them. The ability to do that is phenomenal. Is that easy? For some people it is. It is not easy for everybody. That is the marvelous thing about the Savior. If there is a role model that is great, it is Jesus Christ. He had that ability. No matter what people did, he continued to love them. There is a tremendous amount of power in acquiring that ability.

The next word is success. I will use your role as a child of God as an example because it is your success in that role that this book deals with.

Success: *The successful child of God is willing to do what the unsuccessful child of God is not willing to do.*

Draw a profile of success in whatever you are choosing to improve. If you are willing to do what that profile demands, then you have a credible demand of success. If you are not willing to do that, then it just will not be there. You can't have one without the other.

Next is sacrifice.

Sacrifice: *Giving up something good for something better.*

As you reflect on some of the things you would like to change, what are you willing to give up (sacrifice) to make it happen? As I have studied great men and women from the beginning of time, the common denominator of greatness has been the ability and willingness to sacrifice for whatever they were trying to achieve. When sacrifice has been there, great humans have emerged. Giving up three hours of television a day would be a great sacrifice for some. To be willing to do that, one would have to perceive that the productivity gained in one's personal life would be greater than watching television for those three hours.

Another word is character.

Character: *The ability to carry out a decision after the emotion of making the decision has past.*

This definition will work if you think about it long enough. Several years ago, when I was working in Portland, Oregon, I had a ceremony I went through every morning at nine-thirty. I would leave my office, walk into the lunchroom, and pay homage to a great candy bar machine. I would sink a quarter into that machine and retrieve a *Heath* candy bar. I would take them intravenously if I could.

On one occasion I was putting my quarter into the machine; and from across the room, two colleagues, obviously thinking I could not hear, said to each other, "Hyrum is getting a little porky, don't you think?"

I froze in mid-air, retrieved my quarter, put it in my pocket, and looked over to see who they were. I could have fired both of them. I went back to my office fighting mad. I was all emotionally involved. My wife had been bugging me for about two years to lose twenty-five pounds. I weighed two hundred and twenty-four pounds, about twenty pounds too heavy.

I called Gail on the phone, "Gail, I'm going to lose those twenty-five pounds you've been bugging me about. I'm going to do it. This time I'm going to do it."

I started writing down all the reasons why I should. You know how long it lasted? Eight hours. What happens at the end of eight hours? You get hungry, that's what happens. You go home and walk by the refrigerator and it reaches out and pulls you in and you find yourself sitting on the third shelf eating everything you can get your hands on. *Character is the ability to carry out a decision after the emotion of making that decision has passed.*

One of the emotions you will experience from reading is that you will get a swelling emotion inside that says, "You know, I'm going to do this." Or, "I'm going to do something about that. I can achieve and I'm going to do this."

The very next emotion is, "That's stupid, I can't do that. That's dumb. Why even think about it." Those responses are a result of having been raised in the society in which we live. It says, "Don't try because you might fail, and failure is bad."

A German general said during the Second World War, "No defeat is final; it is only preparation for the next and greater battle." Great concept.

Character, simply stated, is doing what you said you were going to do. If you develop a reputation for that, do you have any idea the effect that has on self-perception? It's immense, just immense. The Savior was a man of character. He did everything he said he was going to do.

The last word is humility.

Humility   *The realization of our dependence on God.*

I have always had strong feelings about that word, regardless of what anyone's background might be. One of the common denominators of greatness is acknowledging that dependence. As power comes from charity, power also comes from knowing who you are, a divine offspring of a divine being.

Now, take these words and plug them into the steps for better self-perception and you'll start looking at yourself differently. Are these definitions part of your character? If not, then you can go back and use this system that I have described in *Eye of Faith*, and specifically identify what you need to change. In a very specific, practical way, do surgery on yourself. Operate on yourself. It all starts with your self-talking and self-thinking.

I bear witness to you that the gospel of Jesus Christ will create change in your life. Just reading about it is not enough. We have to do like the brother of Jared did, and go out and create some rocks. Well, go out and picture yourself the way you want to be; and then every night, take a few moments and see yourself already there. I plead with you to see yourself like the Savior. See yourself, a God managing a world somewhere and your performance will reach your self-image.

Most of all, I hope you will allow it to create changes in *your* life that bring the peace and happiness and security that is only available through a relationship with Jesus Christ.

I am learning to love the sinner and hate the sin because I know that everyone is a child of God.

FIVE COOL PRIESTS

Change for the better occurs only when we set goals and personally commit to a specific plan of action.

Do you know that fewer than 3 percent of the American people are working on a specific set of written goals that really mean something to them? The insurance industry tells us that fewer than five percent of the American people at age sixty-five can put their hands on five thousand dollars in cash. The reason they can't is that they didn't plan to. And sure enough, when they turn sixty-five and open their bankbook, it just isn't there.

We, as a people, are neither establishing goals that mean anything to us nor going after them with all our beings to accomplish them. I look at young people and observe them going through the high school experience. I know some of the goals which could be set, and some of the achievements which could be achieved, and it frightens me that perhaps they are not setting worthy goals.

A Trip to Hawaii

I want you to learn a poem, and I can best describe it to you be telling you the following story.

When I came back from the military, my wife and I came to Brigham Young University to finish our schooling. Instead of settling into one of the student wards, we were assigned to a ward in the metropolis of Orem, which is right next door to Provo.

It has been our practice ever since we were married that, whenever we moved into a new ward, we would immediately go to the bishop and say, "Bishop, we are Hyrum and Gail Smith. We are new in your ward, and we have to have a job in ten days, or we will leave the Church."

That makes bishops very nervous. So, within about a week the bishop came over with his counselors and called us to be Explorer advisor. Now, I say *us* because that calling required *us*. We discovered that is probably the celestial calling in the church.

I was excited about this new calling and went to Mutual that first Wednesday night to meet my boys. I was thinking about all the great things we were going to do, the goals that we were going to set, and all the marvelous things we were going to do. I walked into the classroom.

There sat five cool priests. Have you ever met a cool priest? They were sitting there, and their body language was speaking very loudly; they weren't saying anything with their mouths but their body language spoke. You know what body language is don't you? It is when we speak with our arms and legs. They were sitting there, and one of them had his arms over the back of his chair. What they said to me with their expressions and with their bodies as I walked in was, "I dare you to teach me something!"

I thought to myself as I walked through the door, "Boy, am I in for it." And was I right!

I said, "Brethren, I'm your new Explorer advisor."

I thought they'd be excited about that. They were not. After the opening prayer, I said, "Let me tell you a little bit about me. I'm Hyrum Smith. I was raised in Hawaii, and what a special place it is." After telling them a little bit about Hawaii, I asked, "How would you brethren like to go to Hawaii next year? We'll earn the money together, and I'll show you what to do. We'll put a project together and we'll go and spend two weeks in Hawaii. I know people in the navy—maybe we can go to Pearl Harbor—and we can go to the Church College..."

I was building this great tale about how neat it was going to be for us to go to Hawaii. I thought they would just come off the roof excited. They didn't even flinch. After I finished and started to wind down, I wanted a reaction. I said, "What do you think about that, guys?"

One of them said, "Gee, that's great, Brother Smith. And year after next, we'll go to the moon. Yeah, what do you think about that, Brother Smith?" They laughed me out of the room.

I was devastated. We had a closing prayer and I came home. I described this experience to my wife. I said, "Have you ever met five cool priests? You know, they have long hair, and their shirts are open down to their navels."

The next day I went to one of the brethren I knew in the ward who had had these boys as Scouts. I asked, "You've got to help me. I just got wiped out last night." I told him what had happened and he just laughed.

He said, "Let me tell you something, Brother Smith. Last year those boys had six different Explorer advisors, and every one of them presented some great trip. I will grant you, none of them as ambitious as Hawaii, but they've been promised all kinds of trips, Disneyland, California, and all this stuff; not one of them came through. They didn't go on any of them. So when you came in last night and introduced yourself and said, 'How would you like to go to Hawaii?' it just went off their scope."

I thought about it during the week, so I was ready the next Wednesday. I went back armed for bear. I went into our classroom, and there sat, in the same positions, as if they had slept there for a week, my five cool priests. I sat down. We had our opening prayer.

Then I said, "Brethren, I want to tell you something. Next summer my wife and I are going to Hawaii; and whether any of you go with us or not, I could care less, but we're going. You know what I mean? If you want to go with us, fine. You do what we tell you to do and you can go. Otherwise, forget it."

Well, the body language started to change. The arms came off the chairs. One of them leaned forward on his chair and he looked at me in the eye and said, "You're really serious about this, aren't you, Brother Smith?"

"Yes, I'm very serious about it. Are you interested?"

"Well, yeah. We're interested."

"Let me tell you. If you're interested, there is going to be a strict set of rules you will need to conform to before you can go. The first one is, you've got to memorize a poem."

"Oh, terrific. Let's memorize a poem."

I introduced them that night to the poem. Here it is.

There is no chance, no destiny, no fate that can circumvent or hinder or control the firm resolve of a determined soul.

"What do you think about that poem, brethren?"

"Oh, that's terrific, Brother Smith!"

They didn't know what it meant. The words didn't mean anything to them. But I said, "You're going to learn that poem. We are going to recite it every week. It will be our theme for the next eleven months while we're working on this trip to Hawaii. You will have to recite it, word for word, to the flight attendant when you get on the plane."

I continued, "There are going to be rules; we are going to have a point system. You have to earn a certain number of points to be able to get on the airplane. You can get points by earning money, you can get points by going to all your church meetings, by wearing your uniform to Mutual, and by having a missionary haircut. (Oh, that was a bite!) You can get points for all these things, and the winner is going to get a Centennial Winchester rifle. It is a beautiful weapon."

They started to get a little excited about that. During the next eleven months, we put on twenty-nine major fund-raising projects to earn money to go to Hawaii. About ninety days into this project, we discovered there were not just five cool priests, but there were seventeen. They started coming out of the woodwork.

They would ask the original five, "Are you guys really going to Hawaii?"

"You bet."

"What do you have to do?"

"Learn a poem."

"A poem? Are you kidding?"

"No. We really do."

"All right. Whatever it takes."

They all started to come to meetings. As a result of the excitement of those seventeen guys, we earned the money. We sold everything. We sold pizzas, pies, cuff-links, fire extinguishers, cookies, a cow. One of the members came up missing his boat. We had sold that. We sold everything. These seventeen kids turned into one of the finest sales forces that Orem, Utah, had ever seen.

There was an old bulldozer out in front of the church. In fact, it was just outside the door of the building. It had been there for twelve years. I went to the bishop and said, "Bishop, can we have the bulldozer?"

He said, "What are you going to do with it?"

"Give it to me and the Explorers will sell it."

"It's yours."

I went to another member of the ward who was a welder by trade and asked him, "What would it take to cut up that bulldozer?"

He said, "What do you mean, cut up that bulldozer?"

"Cut it up into little pieces so that we can sell it."

"Do you have any idea how much acetylene it would take to cut up a bulldozer?"

Whatever it takes, you cut it up; and we'll buy your acetylene."

Well, he got intrigued by the idea, so he showed up with his tanks and proceeded to cut this bulldozer up into pieces. All seventeen boys showed up. We borrowed an old septic tank truck from one of the other brethren and hand-loaded the cut-up bulldozer. We sold it and made over six hundred dollars after we paid for the acetylene.

The bishop could not believe it. In fact, he almost asked us for the money because he was having budget problems.

Remember, every Wednesday night while we were going through one fund-raising project after another, they would stand and say, *"There is no chance, no destiny, no fate that can circumvent or hinder or control the firm resolve of a determined soul."*

During the year, I thought it would be great if the boys could sponsor a really classy concert. I went to Brother Reid Nibley at BYU. He is probably one of the finest pianists in the United States; in the world for that matter.

I knocked on Brother Nibley's office door, and said, "Brother Nibley, you don't know who I am, but I know who you are, and I have seventeen Explorers who have never seen a really first-class piano concert. We want to know if you would be willing to put on a benefit concert for us. We are going to Hawaii next summer."

He just laughed and said, "I don't put on benefit concerts for anybody. I am under contract. I just can't do it."

"Brother Nibley, you could do it for us if you wanted to." We talked for a long time and he started to get intrigued about these seventeen boys going to Hawaii. I taught him the poem.

The poem must have had quite an impact because he said, "I'll tell you what, Brother Smith. If you won't tell anybody, I'll do a concert for you."

"I'll only tell the people we sell tickets to."

"You've got a deal."

He became so excited about it, he went to the first violinist of the Utah Symphony, who was Percy Kalt, and said, "Look, these kids are going to Hawaii. How about you coming with me and we will do a first class violin-piano concert for them?"

Percy Kalt got excited, so he came too.

We went out and sold tickets and made seven hundred and fifty dollars on that concert. On that night of the concert, even though these boys had never seen a really first-class concert where really good music is played, they were going to be the ushers. They came all dressed in their Sunday best.

I sat down with them before the concert and said, "Now brethren, this is a first-class concert, a classy concert. This is not your typical ward function. There are no crying babies in a classy concert. Not only that, if people come late, they don't come in during one of the numbers like you're used to. They must wait until the number is over. Then, during the applause, they can sneak in and sit down. There will be no noise, do you understand?"

"Yes sir, there will be no noise."

The concert started. A gracious lady from Orem had brought her baby, and about half-way through the concert, the baby started to cry. Out of nowhere four of my boys appeared in front of this lady, ripped her baby from her arms, and raced out to the foyer with the mother chasing behind.

When they got into the foyer, one of the young men presented the baby back to the lady and said, "Lady, this is classy concert. There are no crying babies in a classy concert."

She learned a great lesson that night, as did these young brethren.

It was a marvelously exciting thing. We would go to the elders' quorum presidency meetings of many of the wards in Orem. We knew they weren't doing their farm projects because the apples weren't getting thinned and picked like they ought to be, so we were hired to do their jobs for them. We would show up at five-thirty Saturday mornings, seventeen of us, really nineteen with my wife and me; and we would thin and pick apples. We did a lot of other things, too.

The boys discovered the power of that poem. The requirement was that they know that poem by heart before they could get into the airplane. The day finally came to go to Hawaii. They all had full uniforms. One of the members of the ward had become emotionally involved in what we were doing and had donated red Explorer jackets. She even embroidered our names on them in nice yellow lettering.

There we were at the Salt Lake airport. All nineteen of us in full uniform. They still talk about that day at the airport, I want you to know. The first boy took his ticket, went up the stairs of the airplane, handed his ticket to the stewardess, and said, "There is no chance, no destiny, no fate that can circumvent or hinder or control the firm resolve of a determined soul. What do you think of that?"

"Oh, that's great, kid."

The next boy went up the stairs, handed her the ticket, and said, "There is no chance, no destiny, no fate that can circumvent or hinder or control the firm resolve of a determined soul." Seventeen times she listened to our poem.

I went up the stairs of the airplane last. I handed her my ticket and she said, "Stop, let me tell you the poem."

I said, "Great!"

She said, "There is no chance, no destiny, no fate that can circumvent or hinder or control the firm resolve of a determined soul."

I said, "Isn't that a great poem?"

She said, "Yes, that's a great poem, and we're thirty minutes late. Would you mind if we left?"

We flew to San Francisco; and on the way, all the flight attendants learned our poem. They memorized it. We arrived in San Francisco and boarded a 747. Between San Francisco and Honolulu all thirteen of the flight attendants memorized the poem. We even said it over the speaker system to all the people on the airplane. By the time we arrived in Hawaii, these boys understood what it meant. They were excited about having established a goal and then being willing to pay the price, whatever it took, to accomplish it.

When we reached Hawaii, we had two marvelous weeks. We were guests of the navy for three days. We were allowed to go out into Pearl Harbor on a destroyer. Boy, did they love that. We went to the Church College of Hawaii and visited the Polynesian Cultural Center. We even stayed with the army for a couple of days. We saw everything, we went swimming, we had a wonderful time.

On one particular day, we went to Pounder's Beach. It is near the temple. That beach earns its name. I discovered that we had probably made a disastrous mistake letting the boys swim there. These kids from Orem had never seen a wave bigger than what they generate in their bathtubs at home. My wife would stand on the beach and count noses, and I was in the water saving lives. Somehow, we got them all back alive.

The most exciting experience that happened was during priesthood meeting. We attended church the weekend we were in Hawaii. Of course, all of us in uniform, red jackets, and missionary haircuts. Whew! They looked like a million dollars. While we were sitting in priesthood meeting, in through the door came another Explorer post from Nevada. They were the *cool* variety. There were about eight of them. They walked in, no uniforms, wild shirts opened to their navel, the hair, and all this cool stuff.

There was an interesting electricity between these two groups. I sat off and watched. They were all really eyeing each other up and down. The Nevada group was wondering who these weirdos from Utah were.

After the meeting they drifted together; and I stood off and listened to the conversation. They were chatting about where they were from and so forth. Finally, one of my boys asked *the* question. "How did you guys *earn* your trip?"

The answer, "What do you mean, earn our trip, man? Our fathers wanted to know if we wanted to go to Hawaii to get us out of their hair for a week, so we came. No big deal."

What happened next was priceless. These seventeen guys of mine gathered around those nine and ate them for lunch.

"What do you mean, you didn't *earn* your trip? Let me tell you how *we* got here." They laid it on them thick and heavy.

Two or three of my boys surprised them by repeating, "There is no chance, no destiny, no fate that can circumvent or hinder or control the firm resolve of a determined soul." It was rewarding to watch the excitement of those seventeen guys drum the others into the ground; *"We earned our trip!"*

Young people, I hope that when you decide to do something, anyone who is aware of the fact that you decided to do it will say, "Consider it done, because so-and-so said he was going to do it."

> *There is no chance, no destiny, no fate that can circumvent or hinder or control the firm resolve of a determined soul.*

What does circumvent mean? Prevent is a good word. What is another way of describing circumvent? Sidestepping. What does hinder mean? Get in the way. Are you beginning to understand what the poem means? What does resolve mean? Determination. When you make a resolve to do something, what do you do? You do it! What is the definition of an obstacle?

> *Obstacle:* *Something that you see when you take your eye off the goal.*

That is what an obstacle is. There are no obstacles if you have the right vision. Most of us live looking down. But every once in a while you have to look up—look at the sky and all the great things that you can do. Then, boom, we're right back looking down. Learn the magic of that poem, and maybe you will start living, and pretty soon you will get up where there aren't any obstacles.

You can do anything you decide you are going to do. For example, last year you didn't do very well in math, so this year you make a firm resolve that you are going to get an A in math. You start working the first part of the year and the mid-term comes. The big exam which is going to determine one-half of your grade in math is tomorrow. But tonight is the big dance and you have a date. Not just with anybody, mind you, this is the one.

What does the poem say, "Nothing is going to get in the way of my resolve to get a good grade."

So you call your friend and say, "Listen, I can't go tonight. Tomorrow is the big test and I'm going to do well in math this year. Maybe next week..." Whew!

Now we know something about firmly resolving to do something. We are all determined souls, hopefully. What are some of the goals we want to set? How about the goal of keeping ourselves morally clean? Hopefully, as we go through Seminary, Sunday School, Primary, and Mutual, and any other meetings, we are taught the difference between right and wrong. If I were to ask the question that would determine whether or not you knew what it meant to be morally clean, not one of you would fail that test. You all know that fornication is wrong, that adultery is wrong, that masturbation is wrong, that petting is wrong; you know that. But for some reason, when you get away from each other's light where it is dark, like the canyon that seems to be by every high school, and you are there with that guy whom you think is pretty neat and the windows are all steamed up, it is too late.

You've got to resolve this now, "Nobody is going to get me into trouble. I am going to keep myself clean and pure."

Do you know why? Because you don't want your future husband, or your future wife, to have the bread that has already had the peanut butter licked off.

Allegory of the Peanut Butter

Have you ever heard the allegory of the peanut butter? On fast Sunday, if somebody would come to me with a piece of my wife's beautiful homemade bread all covered with peanut butter and jelly and say, "How would you like that?" I would probably have broken his arm getting at it. But just as I reach for it, he pulls it back and licks all the peanut butter and jelly off and says, "Here, you can have what is left."

Would you eat it? No! But isn't that what we ask our future spouse to do when we choose to fail in those areas? I hope with all my heart that you make a resolve, if you haven't done so before, "I am going to be clean. I don't care what it costs. I don't care what the popularity cost is (and boy, there is a cost), I am going to keep myself clean."

You young people, keep yourselves clean. The Lord needs you clean. If you haven't decided you are going to be clean and you find yourself having to decide when the temptation is right there in your lap, then it is too late. You have to decide now. Then just follow your own instructions, and you will make it. Everybody knows how to identify what we need to do. Everybody knows how to tell ourselves how to do it. Fewer than 3 percent have the character to do it. I plead with you young people to be part of that 3 percent. Will you? Will you remember that first poem?

> There is no chance, no destiny, no fate that can circumvent or hinder or control the firm resolve of a determined soul.

I know that Jesus Christ lives. I know that He loves us. I know He knows who we are. He knows who you are. He knows what your weaknesses are. He stands pleading with you to consider the alternatives, to say to yourself, "What do I win, if I go this direction? If

I am presented with drugs, what do I win if I gain the thing I seek? A dream, a breath, a froth, a fleeting temporary joy? Who buys a minute's mirth to wail a week or a year or ten?"

I am enjoying success in my resolve to change for the better because I am setting goals and writing affirmations.

POSTSCRIPT

This book would not be complete without adding this postscript. I have discussed principles which I feel are essential to our implementing change successfully in our lives. These principles have been exemplified in the life of the Savior as he fulfilled his mission in morality.

The Savior knew who he was and so acted upon that knowledge. At an early age, he began to go about his Father's business. There were no doubts in his mind who he was when he responded to Satan's tempting question, "If you are the Son of God..."

The Savior prepared himself so that he would and could pay attention to the cues which came to him because of his eternal heritage. He went into the wilderness and fasted before he began his mission. He built upon what he had been given and, as Luke recorded, "increased in wisdom and stature, and in favour with God and man."

The Savior's unwavering obedience to the will of his Father is what made it possible for him to become the author of eternal salvation. He was tempted in all things and came through unscathed from sin. At the time of his greatest test, he went to the source of his and our greatest strength—the Father.

The Savior's love is named charity because he, better than anyone, can love the sinner and hate the sin. Time and time again, he gave forth his love to those who disobeyed or who had despitefully used him.

The Savior stood firm to his mission and to his heritage. His firm resolve is a testimony to us all. He also realized his relationship with his Father. He knew the power that came to him because of his obedience, faith, love, and willingness to share with others that which had been given him by the Father.

The Savior has promised he will give all that he has been given by the Father to those who willingly give obedience, show faith and charity, and share with others their testimonies, time, talents, and worldly goods so that the kingdom of God may be built up upon the earth.

My young people, I hope and pray that you may implement into your lives these principles of the Savior and realize the power which comes from them. If you can, the time spent in reading this book will be well spent.